THE C PUZZLE BOOK

PRENTICE HALL SOFTWARE SERIES

Brian W. Kernighan, advisor

THE C PUZZLE BOOK

Second Edition

Alan R. Feuer

PRENTICE HALL, Englewood Cliffs, New Jersey 07632

Library of Congress Cataloging-in-Publication Data

FEUER, ALAN R.
  The C puzzle book—2nd ed.
    1. C (Computer program language) 2. UNIX
(Computer operating system) I. Title.
QA76.73.C15F48 1989   005.13'3   89-3561
ISBN 0-13-115502-4

Editorial/production supervision: *Patrice Fraccio*
Cover design: *Photo Plus Art*
Manufacturing buyer: *Mary Noonan*

 © 1989 by Bell Laboratories, Incorporated
Published by Prentice-Hall, Inc.
A Division of Simon & Schuster
Englewood Cliffs, New Jersey 07632

The author and publisher of this book have used their best efforts in preparing
this book. These efforts include the development, research, and testing of the
theories and programs to determine their effectiveness. The author and
publisher make no warranty of any kind, expressed or implied, with regard to
these programs or the documentation contained in this book. The author and
publisher shall not be liable in any event for incidental or consequential
damages in connection with, or arising out of, the furnishing, performance, or
use of these programs.

Printed in the United States of America
10 9 8 7 6 5 4

ISBN   0-13-115502-4

Prentice-Hall International (UK) Limited, *London*
Prentice-Hall of Australia Pty. Limited, *Sydney*
Prentice-Hall Canada Inc., *Toronto*
Prentice-Hall Hispanoamericana, S.A., *Mexico*
Prentice-Hall of India Private Limited, *New Delhi*
Prentice-Hall of Japan, Inc., *Tokyo*
Simon & Schuster Asia Pte. Ltd., *Singapore*
Editora Prentice-Hall do Brasil, Ltda., *Rio de Janeiro*

CONTENTS

Preface ....page vii

PUZZLES

Operators..page 3

    1. Basic Arithmetic Operators 5

    2. Assignment Operators 7

    3. Logic and Increment Operators 9

    4. Bitwise Operators 11

    5. Relational and Conditional Operators 13

    6. Operator Precedence and Evaluation 15

Basic Types...page 17

    1. Character, String, and Integer Types 19

    2. Integer and Floating Point Casts 21

    3. More Casts 23

Included Files..page 25

Control Flow ....page 27

    1. `if` Statement 29

    2. `while` and `for` Statements 31

    3. Statement Nesting 33

    4. `switch`, `break`, and `continue` 35 _GO OVER_

Programming Style _SKIP_ ....page 37

    1. Choose the Right Condition 39

    2. Choose the Right Construct 41

Storage Classes ....page 43

    1. Blocks 45

    2. Functions 47

3. More Functions 49

4. Files 51

Pointers and Arrays..page 53

1. Simple Pointer and Array 55

2. Array of Pointers 57

3. Multidimensional Array 59

4. Pointer Stew 61

Structures ....page 63

1. Simple Structure, Nested Structure 65

2. Array of Structures 67

3. Array of Pointers to Structures 69

Preprocessor...page 71

1. The Preprocessor Knows Little C 73

2. Caution Pays 75

SOLUTIONS

Operators..page 79

Basic Types..page 100

Control Flow ....page 108

Programming Style ....page 120

Storage Classes ....page 125

Pointers and Arrays..page 133

Structures ....page 145

Preprocessor..page 162

APPENDICES

1. Precedence Table ....page 169

2. Operator Summary Table..page 171

3. ASCII Table...page 177

4. Type Hierarchy Chart ....page 179

PREFACE

C is not a large language. Measured by the weight of its reference manual, C could even be classified as small. The small size reflects a lack of confining rules rather than a lack of power. Users of C learn early to appreciate the elegance of expression afforded by its clear design.

Such elegance might seem needlessly arcane for new C programmers. The lack of restrictions means that C programs can be and are written with full-bodied expressions that may appear as printing errors to the novice. The cohesiveness of C often admits clear, but terse, ways to express common programming tasks.

The process of learning C, as for any programming language, may be modeled by three steps (no doubt repeated many times over). Step one is to understand the language syntax, at least to the point where the translator no longer complains of meaningless constructions. Step two is to know what meaning the translator will ascribe to properly formed constructions. And step three is to develop a programming style fitting for the language; it is the art of writing clear, concise, and correct programs.

The puzzles in this book are designed to help the reader through the second step. They will challenge the reader's mastery of the basic rules of C and lead the reader into seldom reached corners, beyond reasonable limits, and past a few open pits. (Yes, C, as all real languages, has its share of obscurities that are learned by experience.)

The puzzles should *not* be read as samples of good coding; indeed, some of the code is atrocious. But this is to be expected. Often the same qualities that make a program poor make a puzzle interesting:

- ambiguity of expression, requiring a rule book to interpret;
- complexity of structure, data and program structure not easily kept in one's head;
- obscurity of usage, using concepts in nonstandard ways.

The puzzles in this book are based on ANSI Standard C. Depending upon the vintage of your local compiler, some of the features explored here may not be implemented. Fortunately, ANSI C is a superset of most implementations of C so it is very unlikely that your compiler will have a feature implemented in a different way than described here.

HOW TO USE THIS BOOK

The C Puzzle Book is a workbook intended to be used with a C language textbook such as *The C Programming Language* by Brian Kernighan and Dennis Ritchie (Prentice-Hall, 1988) or *The C Trainer* by Alan Feuer (Prentice-Hall, 1986). This book is divided into sections with one major topic per section. Each section comprises C programs that explore different aspects of the section topic. The programs are sprinkled with print statements. The primary task is to discover what each program prints. All of the programs are independent of one another, though the later puzzles assume that you understand the properties of C illustrated in earlier puzzles.

The output for each program is given on the page following the text of the program. Each of the programs was run from the text under the UNIX Operating System on a Sun 3 Workstation and under MS/DOS on an IBM PC/AT computer. For the few cases where the output is different on the two machines, output is given from both.

The larger portion of the book is devoted to step-by-step derivations of the puzzle solutions. Many of the derivations are accompanied by tips and caveats for programming in C.

A typical scenario for using the puzzles might go like this:

- Read about a topic in the language textbook.
- For each program in the puzzle book section on the topic
  - Work the puzzles of the program.
  - Compare your answers to the program output.
  - Read the solution derivations.

ACKNOWLEDGEMENTS

The first C puzzles were developed for an introductory C programming course that I taught at Bell Laboratories. The encouraging response from students led me to hone the puzzles and embellish the solutions. A number of my friends and colleagues have given valuable comments and corrections to various drafts of this book. They are Al Boysen, Jr., Jeannette Feuer, Brian Kernighan, John Linderman, David Nowitz, Elaine Piskorik, Bill Roome, Keith Vollherbst, and Charles Wetherell. Finally, I am grateful for the fruitful environment and generous support provided me by Bell Laboratories.

Alan Feuer

THE C PUZZLE BOOK

PUZZLES

Operators

1. Basic Arithmetic Operators

2. Assignment Operators

3. Logic and Increment Operators

4. Bitwise Operators

5. Relational and Conditional Operators

6. Operator Precedence and Evaluation

C programs are built from statements, statements from expressions, and expressions from operators and operands. C is unusually rich in operators; see the operator summary in Appendix 2 if you need convincing. Because of this richness, the rules that determine how operators apply to operands play a central role in the understanding of expressions. The rules, known as *precedence* and *associativity*, are summarized in the precedence table of Appendix 1. Use the table to solve the problems in this section.

Operators 1: Basic Arithmetic Operators

What does the following program print?

```
main()
{
    int x;

    x = - 3 + 4 * 5 - 6; printf("%d\n",x);         (Operators 1.1)
    x = 3 + 4 % 5 - 6; printf("%d\n",x);           (Operators 1.2)
    x = - 3 * 4 % - 6 / 5; printf("%d\n",x);       (Operators 1.3)
    x = ( 7 + 6 ) % 5 / 2; printf("%d\n",x);       (Operators 1.4)
}
```

Operators 1: Basic Arithmetic Operators

OUTPUT

11	*(Operators 1.1)*
1	*(Operators 1.2)*
0	*(Operators 1.3)*
1	*(Operators 1.4)*

Derivations begin on page 79.

Operators 2: Assignment Operators

What does the following program print?

```
#define PRINTX printf("%d\n",x)

main()
{
    int x=2, y, z;

    x *= 3 + 2; PRINTX;                    (Operators 2.1)
    x *= y = z = 4; PRINTX;                (Operators 2.2)
    x = y == z; PRINTX;                    (Operators 2.3)
    x == ( y = z ); PRINTX;               (Operators 2.4)
}
```

Operators 2: Assignment Operators

OUTPUT

10	*(Operators 2.1)*
40	*(Operators 2.2)*
1	*(Operators 2.3)*
1	*(Operators 2.4)*

Derivations begin on page 82.

Operators 3: Logic and Increment Operators

What does the following program print?

```
#define PRINT(int) printf("%d\n",int)

main()
{
    int x, y, z;

    x = 2; y = 1; z = 0;
    x = x && y || z; PRINT(x);                (Operators 3.1)
    PRINT( x || ! y && z );                   (Operators 3.2)

    x = y = 1;
    z = x ++ - 1; PRINT(x); PRINT(z);         (Operators 3.3)
    z += - x ++ + ++ y; PRINT(x); PRINT(z);   (Operators 3.4)
    z = x / ++ x; PRINT(z);                   (Operators 3.5)
}
```

Operators 3: Logic and Increment Operators

OUTPUT

1	*(Operators 3.1)*
1	*(Operators 3.2)*
2	*(Operators 3.3)*
0	
3	*(Operators 3.4)*
0	
?	*(Operators 3.5)*

Derivations begin on page 85.

Operators 4: Bitwise Operators

What does the following program print?   *FORMAL PARAMETER*

```
#define PRINT(int) printf(#int " = %d\n",int)

main()
{
    int x, y, z;

    x = 03; y = 02; z = 01;
    PRINT( x | y & z );                           (Operators 4.1)
    PRINT( x | y & ~ z );                          (Operators 4.2)
    PRINT( x ^ y & ~ z );                          (Operators 4.3)
    PRINT( x & y && z );                           (Operators 4.4)

    x = 1; y = -1;
    PRINT( ! x | x );                              (Operators 4.5)
    PRINT( ~ x | x );                              (Operators 4.6)
    PRINT( x ^ x );                                (Operators 4.7)
    x <<= 3; PRINT(x);                             (Operators 4.8)
    y <<= 3; PRINT(y);                             (Operators 4.9)
    y >>= 3; PRINT(y);                            (Operators 4.10)
}
```

Operators 4: Bitwise Operators

OUTPUT

`x	y & z = 3`	*(Operators 4.1)*
`x	y & ~ z = 3`	*(Operators 4.2)*
`x ^ y & ~ z = 1`	*(Operators 4.3)*
`x & y && z = 1`	*(Operators 4.4)*
`! x	x = 1`	*(Operators 4.5)*
`~ x	x = -1`	*(Operators 4.6)*
`x ^ x = 0`	*(Operators 4.7)*
`x = 8`	*(Operators 4.8)*
`y = -8`	*(Operators 4.9)*
`y = ?`	*(Operators 4.10)*

Derivations begin on page 89.

Operators 5: Relational and Conditional Operators

What does the following program print?

```
#define PRINT(int) printf(#int " = %d\n",int)

main()
{
    int x=1, y=1, z=1;

    x += y += z;
    PRINT( x < y ? y : x );                     (Operators 5.1)

    PRINT( x < y ? x ++ : y ++ );
    PRINT(x); PRINT(y);                         (Operators 5.2)

    PRINT( z += x < y ? x ++ : y ++ );
    PRINT(y); PRINT(z);                         (Operators 5.3)

    x = 3; y = z = 4;
    PRINT( (z >= y >= x) ? 1 : 0 );             (Operators 5.4)
    PRINT( z >= y && y >= x );                  (Operators 5.5)
}
```

Operators 5: Relational and Conditional Operators

OUTPUT

```
x < y ? y : x = 3                        (Operators 5.1)
x < y ? x ++ : y ++ = 2                  (Operators 5.2)
x = 3
y = 3
z += x < y ? x ++ : y ++ = 4             (Operators 5.3)
y = 4
z = 4
(z >= y >= x) ? 1 : 0 = 0                (Operators 5.4)
z >= y && y >= x = 1                     (Operators 5.5)
```

Derivations begin on page 94.

Operators 6: Operator Precedence and Evaluation

What does the following program print?

```
#define PRINT3(x,y,z) \
        printf(#x "=%d\t" #y "=%d\t" #z "=%d\n",x,y,z)

main()
{
    int x, y, z;

    x = y = z = 1;
    ++x || ++y && ++z; PRINT3(x,y,z);              (Operators 6.1)


    x = y = z = 1;
    ++x && ++y || ++z; PRINT3(x,y,z);              (Operators 6.2)


    x = y = z = 1;
    ++x && ++y && ++z; PRINT3(x,y,z);              (Operators 6.3)


    x = y = z = -1;
    ++x && ++y || ++z; PRINT3(x,y,z);              (Operators 6.4)


    x = y = z = -1;
    ++x || ++y && ++z; PRINT3(x,y,z);              (Operators 6.5)


    x = y = z = -1;
    ++x && ++y && ++z; PRINT3(x,y,z);              (Operators 6.6)
}
```

Operators 6: Operator Precedence and Evaluation

OUTPUT

x=2	y=1	z=1	*(Operators 6.1)*
x=2	y=2	z=1	*(Operators 6.2)*
x=2	y=2	z=2	*(Operators 6.3)*
x=0	y=-1	z=0	*(Operators 6.4)*
x=0	y=0	z=-1	*(Operators 6.5)*
x=0	y=-1	z=-1	*(Operators 6.6)*

Derivations begin on page 97.

Basic Types

1. Character, String, and Integer Types

2. Integral and Floating Point Casts

3. More Casts

C has a comparatively small set of built-in types. The arithmetic types may be blindly mixed in expressions, the results governed by a simple hierarchy of conversions. This hierarchy is illustrated in Appendix 4.

For some of the puzzles in this section you will need to know the corresponding integer value of some characters. The tables in Appendix 3 show the values for the characters in the ASCII set. A few of the puzzles yield a different result on the Intel 8086 than on the Motorola 68000. For those puzzles, output from both machines is given.

Basic Types 1: Character, String, and Integer Types

What does the following program print?

```
#include <stdio.h>

#define PRINT(format,x) printf(#x " =  %" #format "\n",x)

int    integer = 5;
char   character = '5';
char   *string = "5";

main()
{
   PRINT(d,string); PRINT(d,character); PRINT(d,integer);
   PRINT(s,string); PRINT(c,character); PRINT(c,integer=53);
   PRINT(d, ( '5'>5 ));                          (Basic Types 1.1)

      {
         int x = -2;
         unsigned int ux = -2;

         PRINT(o,x); PRINT(o,ux);
         PRINT(d,x/2); PRINT(d,ux/2);
         PRINT(o,x>>1); PRINT(o,ux>>1);
         PRINT(d,x>>1); PRINT(d,ux>>1);         (Basic Types 1.2)
      }
}
```

Basic Types 1: Character, String, and Integer Types

OUTPUT

```
string = an address                              (Basic Types 1.1)
character = 53
integer = 5
string = 5
character = 5
integer=53 = 5
( '5'>5 ) = 1


x = 177776                                  (Basic Types 1.2-Intel 8086)
ux = 177776
x/2 = -1
ux/2 = 32767
x>>1 = 177777 or 77777
ux>>1 = 77777
x>>1 = -1 or 32767
ux>>1 = 32767


x = 37777777776                          (Basic Types 1.2-Motorola 68000)
ux = 37777777776
x/2 = -1
ux/2 = 2147483647
x>>1 = 37777777777 or 17777777777
ux>>1 = 3777777777
x>>1 = -1 or 2147483647
ux>>1 = 2147483647
```

Derivations begin on page 100.

Basic Types 2: Integer and Floating Point Casts

What does the following program print?

```
#include <stdio.h>

#define PR(x) printf(#x " = %.8g\t",(double)x)
#define NL putchar('\n')
#define PRINT4(x1,x2,x3,x4) PR(x1); PR(x2); PR(x3); PR(x4); NL

main()
{
    double d;
    float f;
    long l;
    int i;

    i = l = f = d = 100/3; PRINT4(i,l,f,d);          (Basic Types 2.1)
    d = f = l = i = 100/3; PRINT4(i,l,f,d);          (Basic Types 2.2)
    i = l = f = d = 100/3.; PRINT4(i,l,f,d);         (Basic Types 2.3)
    d = f = l = i = (float)100/3;
       PRINT4(i,l,f,d);                              (Basic Types 2.4)

    i = l = f = d = (double)(100000/3);
    PRINT4(i,l,f,d);                                 (Basic Types 2.5)
    d = f = l = i = 100000/3;
    PRINT4(i,l,f,d);                                 (Basic Types 2.6)
}
```

(handwritten annotation) INTEGER DIVIDED BY AN INTEGER IS ALWAYS AN INTEGER

Basic Types 2: Integer and Floating Point Casts

OUTPUT

```
i = 33   l = 33   f = 33   d = 33                        (Basic Types 2.1)
i = 33   l = 33   f = 33   d = 33                        (Basic Types 2.2)
i = 33   l = 33   f = 33.333332   d = 33.333333          (Basic Types 2.3)
i = 33   l = 33   f = 33   d = 33                        (Basic Types 2.4)


i = overflow   l = 33333   f = 33333   d = 33333
                                                 (Basic Types 2.5-Intel 8086)
i = overflow   l = -32203   f = -32203   d = -32203
                                                 (Basic Types 2.6-Intel 8086)


i = 33333   l = 33333   f = 33333   d = 33333
                                              (Basic Types 2.5-Motorola 68000)
i = 33333   l = 33333   f = 33333   d = 33333
                                              (Basic Types 2.6-Motorola 68000)
```

Derivations begin on page 102.

Basic Types 3: More Casts

What does the following program print?

```
#include <stdio.h>

#define PR(x) printf(#x " = %g\t",(double)(x))
#define NL putchar('\n')
#define PRINT1(x1) PR(x1); NL
#define PRINT2(x1,x2) PR(x1); PRINT1(x2)

main()
{
    double d=3.2, x;
    int i=2, y;

    x = (y=d/i)*2; PRINT2(x,y);              (Basic Types 3.1)
    y = (x=d/i)*2; PRINT2(x,y);              (Basic Types 3.2)

    y = d * (x=2.5/d); PRINT1(y);            (Basic Types 3.3)
    x = d * (y = ((int)2.9+1.1)/d); PRINT2(x,y);  (Basic Types 3.4)
}
```

Basic Types 3: More Casts

OUTPUT

x = 2	y = 1	*(Basic Types 3.1)*
x = 1.6	y = 3	*(Basic Types 3.2)*
y = 2		*(Basic Types 3.3)*
x = 0	y = 0	*(Basic Types 3.4)*

Derivations begin on page 106.

Included Files

Each of the remaining programs in this book begins with the preprocessor statement

```
#include "defs.h"
```

When the programs are compiled, the preprocessor replaces this line with the contents of the file defs.h, making the definitions in defs.h available for use. Here is a listing of defs.h:

```
#include <stdio.h>

#define PR(fmt,val) printf(#val " = %" #fmt "\t",(val))
#define NL putchar('\n')

#define PRINT1(f,x1)  PR(f,x1), NL
#define PRINT2(f,x1,x2)  PR(f,x1), PRINT1(f,x2)
#define PRINT3(f,x1,x2,x3)  PR(f,x1), PRINT2(f,x2,x3)
#define PRINT4(f,x1,x2,x3,x4)  PR(f,x1), PRINT3(f,x2,x3,x4)
```

defs.h begins with an include statement of its own, calling for the insertion of the file stdio.h, as required by the standard C library. The rest of defs.h comprises macros for printing. As an example, to print 5 as a decimal number, the PRINT1 macro could be called by the expression

```
PRINT1(d,5)
```

which expands to

```
PR(d,5), NL
```

which further expands to

```
printf(#5 " = %" #d "\t",(5)), putchar('\n')
```

which finally becomes

```
printf("5 = %d\t",(5)), putchar('\n')
```

Control Flow

1. `if` Statement

2. `while` and `for` Statements

3. Statement Nesting

4. `switch`, `break`, and `continue`

C, as most programming languages, has control constructs for conditional selection and looping. To work the puzzles in this section, you will need to know how to determine the extent of each construct. In a well-formatted program, extent is indicated by indentation. Reading a poorly-formatted program is difficult and error prone; the following puzzles should convince you.

Control Flow 1: if Statement

What does the following program print?

```
#include "defs.h"

main()
{
    int x, y=1, z;

    if( y!=0 ) x=5;
    PRINT1(d,x);                              (Control Flow 1.1)

    if( y==0 ) x=3;
    else x=5;
    PRINT1(d,x);                              (Control Flow 1.2)

    x=1;
    if( y<0 ) if( y>0 ) x=3;
    else x=5;
    PRINT1(d,x);                              (Control Flow 1.3)

    if( z=y<0 ) x=3;
    else if( y==0 ) x=5;
    else x=7;
    PRINT2(d,x,z);                            (Control Flow 1.4)

    if( z=(y==0) ) x=5;
    x=3;
    PRINT2(d,x,z);                            (Control Flow 1.5)

    if( x=z=y ); x=3;
    PRINT2(d,x,z);                            (Control Flow 1.6)
}
```

Control Flow 1: if Statement

OUTPUT

x = 5			*(Control Flow 1.1)*
x = 5			*(Control Flow 1.2)*
x = 1			*(Control Flow 1.3)*
x = 7	z = 0		*(Control Flow 1.4)*
x = 3	z = 0		*(Control Flow 1.5)*
x = 3	z = 1		*(Control Flow 1.6)*

Derivations begin on page 108.

Control Flow 2: While and for Statements

What does the following program print?

```
#include "defs.h"

main()
{
    int x, y, z;

    x=y=0;
    while( y<10 ) ++y; x += y;
    PRINT2(d,x,y);                              (Control Flow 2.1)


    x=y=0;
    while( y<10 ) x += ++y;
    PRINT2(d,x,y);                              (Control Flow 2.2)


    y=1;
    while( y<10 ) {
        x = y++; z = ++y;
    }
    PRINT3(d,x,y,z);                            (Control Flow 2.3)



    for( y=1; y<10; y++ ) x=y;
    PRINT2(d,x,y);                              (Control Flow 2.4)


    for( y=1; (x=y)<10; y++ ) ;
    PRINT2(d,x,y);                              (Control Flow 2.5)


    for( x=0,y=1000; y>1; x++,y/=10 )
        PRINT2(d,x,y);                          (Control Flow 2.6)
}
```

Control Flow 2: while and for Statements

OUTPUT

x = 10	y = 10		*(Control Flow 2.1)*
x = 55	y = 10		*(Control Flow 2.2)*
x = 9	y = 11	z = 11	*(Control Flow 2.3)*
x = 9	y = 10		*(Control Flow 2.4)*
x = 10	y = 10		*(Control Flow 2.5)*
x = 0	y = 1000		*(Control Flow 2.6)*
x = 1	y = 100		
x = 2	y = 10		

Derivations begin on page 111.

Control Flow 3: Statement Nesting

What does the following program print?

```
#include "defs.h"
#define ENUF 3
#define EOS '\0'
#define NEXT(i) input[i++]
#define FALSE 0
#define TRUE 1
char input[]="PI=3.14159, approximately";

main()
{
   char c;
   int done, high, i, in, low;

   i=low=in=high=0;
   while( c=NEXT(i) != EOS )
      if( c<'0' ) low++;
      else if( c>'9' ) high++;
      else in++;
   PRINT3(d,low,in,high);                        (Control Flow 3.1)

   i=low=in=high=0; done=FALSE;
   while( (c=NEXT(i))!=EOS && !done )
      if( c<'0' ) low++;
      else if( c>'9' ) high++;
      else in++;
      if( low>=ENUF || high>=ENUF || in>=ENUF ) done=TRUE;
   PRINT3(d,low,in,high);                        (Control Flow 3.2)

   i=low=in=high=0; done=FALSE;
   while( (c=NEXT(i))!=EOS && !done )
      if( c<'0' ) done = (++low==ENUF ? TRUE : FALSE) ;
      else if( c>'9' ) done = (++high==ENUF ? TRUE : FALSE);
      else done = (++in==ENUF ? TRUE : FALSE);
   PRINT3(d,low,in,high);                        (Control Flow 3.3)
}
```

Control Flow 3: Statement Nesting

OUTPUT

low = 25	in = 0	high = 0	*(Control Flow 3.1)*
low = 3	in = 6	high = 16	*(Control Flow 3.2)*
low = 0	in = 0	high = 3	*(Control Flow 3.3)*

Derivations begin on page 115.

Control Flow 4: `switch`, `break`, and `continue`

What does the following program print?

```c
#include "defs.h"

char input[] = "SSSWILTECH1\1\11W\1WALLMP1";

main()
{
    int i, c;

    for( i=2; (c=input[i]) !='\0'; i++) {
        switch(c) {
        case 'a':   putchar('i'); continue;
        case '1':   break;
        case 1:     while( (c=input[++i]) !='\1' && c!='0' ) ;
        case 9:     putchar('S');
        case 'E':
        case 'L':   continue;
        default:    putchar(c);
                    continue;
        }
        putchar(' ');
    }
    putchar('\n');                                    (Control Flow 4.1)
}
```

Control Flow 4: `switch`, `break`, and `continue`

OUTPUT

`SWITCH SWAMP`   *(Control Flow 4.1)*

Derivation begins on page 117.

Programming Style

1. Choose the Right Condition

2. Choose the Right Construct

Much has been written about programming style, about which constructs to avoid and which to imitate. A cursory conclusion from the seemingly diverse advice is that good style is largely a matter of personal taste. A more reasoned conclusion is that good style in programming, as elsewhere, is a matter of good judgement. And while there are many good style guidelines, there are few always appropriate, always applicable style rules.

With this in mind, the following puzzles illustrate a few common style blunders. The solutions given are not so much answers, as in other sections, but rather alternatives. If there is an overall key to good style, it is a recognition of the final two steps in writing a readable program:

- Establish a clear statement of the idea to be coded.

- Develop the structure of the code from the structure of the idea statement.

Programming Style 1: Choose the Right Condition

Improve the following program fragments through reorganization.

```
while(A) {
    if(B) continue;
    C;
}                                        (Programming Style 1.1)

do {
    if(!A) continue;
    else B;
    C;
} while(A);                              (Programming Style 1.2)

if(A)
    if(B)
        if(C) D;
        else;
    else;
else
    if(B)
        if(C) E;
        else F;
    else;
}                                        (Programming Style 1.3)

while( (c=getchar())!='\n' ) {
    if( c==' ' ) continue;
    if( c=='\t' ) continue;
    if( c<'0' ) return(OTHER);
    if( c<='9' ) return(DIGIT);
    if( c<'a' ) return(OTHER);
    if( c<='z' ) return(ALPHA);
    return(OTHER);
} return(EOL);                           (Programming Style 1.4)
```

Programming Style 1: Choose the Right Condition

Derivations begin on page 120.

Programming Style 2: Choose the Right Construct

Improve the following program fragments through reorganization.

```
done = i = 0;
while( i<MAXI && !done ) {
    if( (x/=2)>1 ) { i++; continue; }
    done++;
}                                        (Programming Style 2.1)
```

```
plusflg = zeroflg = negflg = 0;
if( a>0 ) ++plusflg;
if( a==0 ) ++zeroflg;
else if( !plusflg ) ++negflg;            (Programming Style 2.2)
```

```
if(A) { B; return; }
if(C) { D; return; }
if(E) { F; return; }
G; return;
                                         (Programming Style 2.3)
```

```
i=0;
while((c=getchar())!=EOF){
if(c!='\n'||c!='\t'){s[i++]=c;continue;}
if(c=='\n')break;
if(c=='\t')c=' ';
s[i++]=c;}                               (Programming Style 2.4)
```

```
if( x!=0 )
    if( j>k ) y=j/x;
    else y=k/x;
else
    if( j>k ) y=j/NEARZERO;
    else y=k/NEARZERO;
}                                        (Programming Style 2.5)
```

Programming Style 2: Choose the Right Construct

Derivations begin on page 122.

Storage Classes

1. Blocks

2. Functions

3. More Functions

4. Files

Each variable in C possesses three fundamental properties: type, scope, and lifetime. The type of a variable determines the amount of storage occupied by the variable and the operations permissible on the variable. Type was covered in an earlier chapter.

The *scope* of a variable is that part of a program text in which the variable name is visible. Scope is controlled by the location of declarations. The boundaries of scope are blocks, functions, and files.

Lifetime is the portion of a program execution during which a variable has a value. Lifetime is controlled by storage class.

Storage Classes 1: Blocks

What does the following program print?

```
#include "defs.h"

int i=0;

main()
{
    auto int i=1;
    PRINT1(d,i);
    {
        int i=2;
        PRINT1(d,i);
        {
            i += 1;
            PRINT1(d,i);
        }
        PRINT1(d,i);
    }
    PRINT1(d,i);
}
```

(Storage Classes 1.1)

Storage Classes 1: Blocks

OUTPUT

```
i = 1       (Storage Classes 1.1)
i = 2
i = 3
i = 3
i = 1
```

Derivations begin on page 125.

Storage Classes 2: Functions

What does the following program print?

```
#include "defs.h"

#define LOW 0
#define HIGH 5
#define CHANGE 2
void workover();

int i=LOW;

main()
{
    auto int i=HIGH;
    reset( i/2 ); PRINT1(d,i);
    reset( i=i/2 ); PRINT1(d,i);
    i = reset( i/2 ); PRINT1(d,i);

    workover(i); PRINT1(d,i);                    (Storage Classes 2.1)
}

void workover(int i)
{
    i = (i%i) * ((i*i)/(2*i) + 4);
    PRINT1(d,i);
}

int reset(int i)
{
    i = i<=CHANGE ? HIGH : LOW;
    return(i);
}
```

Storage Classes 2: Functions

OUTPUT

```
i = 5        (Storage Classes 2.1)
i = 2
i = 5
i = 0
i = 5
```

Derivations begin on page 127.

Storage Classes 3: More Functions

What does the following program print?

```c
#include "defs.h"

int i=1;

main()
{
    auto int i, j;
    i = reset();
    for( j=1; j<=3; j++ ) {
        PRINT2(d,i,j);
        PRINT1(d,next(i));
        PRINT1(d,last(i));
        PRINT1(d,new(i+j));
    }
}

int reset(void)
{
    return(i);
}

int next(int j)
{
    return( j=i++ );
}

int last(int j)
{
    static int i=10;
    return( j=i-- );
}

int new(int i)
{
    auto int j=10;
    return( i=j+=i );
```

(Storage Classes 3.1)

Storage Classes 3: More Functions

OUTPUT

```
i = 1     j = 1        (Storage Classes 3.1)
next(i) = 1
last(i) = 10
new(i+j) = 12
i = 1     j = 2
next(i) = 2
last(i) = 9
new(i+j) = 13
i = 1     j = 3
next(i) = 3
last(i) = 8
new(i+j) = 14
```

Derivations begin on page 129.

Storage Classes 4: Files

What does the following program print?

```
#include "defs.h"
int i=1;

main()
{
    auto int i, j;

    i = reset();
    for( j=1; j<=3; j++ ) {
        PRINT2(d,i,j);
        PRINT1(d,next());
        PRINT1(d,last());
        PRINT1(d,new(i+j));
    }
}
```

(Storage Classes 4.1)

In another file

```
static int i=10;

next(void)
{
    return( i+=1 );
}

last(void)
{
    return( i-=1 );
}

new(int i)
{
    static int j=5;
    return( i=j+=i );
}
```

In yet another file

```
extern int i;

int reset(void)
{
    return(i);
}
```

Storage Classes 4: Files

OUTPUT

```
i = 1     j = 1     (Storage Classes 4.1)
next() = 11
last() = 10
new(i+j) = 7
i = 1     j = 2
next() = 11
last() = 10
new(i+j) = 10
i = 1     j = 3
next() = 11
last() = 10
new(i+j) = 14
```

Derivations begin on page 131.

Pointers and Arrays

1. Simple Pointer and Array

2. Array of Pointers

3. Multidimensional Array

4. Pointer Stew

Pointers have long been maligned in style guides for making programs more difficult to read and thus more difficult to write without errors. By their nature, it is impossible to identify fully a pointer's referent without backing up to where the pointer was last defined; this adds complexity to a program.

The C language, rather than restricting the use of pointers, often makes them the natural choice for use. As the following puzzles will illustrate, pointers and arrays are very closely related. For any application using array indexing, a pointer version also exists. The warnings about the dangers of pointers apply as strongly to C as to any language.

Pointers and Arrays 1: Simple Pointer and Array

What does the following program print?

```
#include "defs.h"

int a[] = { 0, 1, 2, 3, 4 };

main()
{
    int i, *p;

    for( i=0; i<=4; i++ ) PR(d,a[i]);          (Pointers and Arrays 1.1)
    NL;
    for( p= &a[0]; p<=&a[4]; p++)
        PR(d,*p);                               (Pointers and Arrays 1.2)
    NL; NL;

    for( p= &a[0],i=1; i<=5; i++)
        PR(d,p[i]);                             (Pointers and Arrays 1.3)
    NL;
    for( p=a,i=0; p+i<=a+4; p++,i++)
        PR(d,*(p+i));                           (Pointers and Arrays 1.4)
    NL; NL;

    for( p=a+4; p>=a; p--) PR(d,*p);           (Pointers and Arrays 1.5)
    NL;
    for( p=a+4,i=0; i<=4; i++)
        PR(d,p[-i]);                            (Pointers and Arrays 1.6)
    NL;
    for( p=a+4; p>=a; p--) PR(d,a[p-a]);       (Pointers and Arrays 1.7)
    NL;
}
```

Pointers and Arrays 1: Simple Pointer and Array

OUTPUT

```
a[i] = 0     a[i] = 1     a[i] = 2     a[i] = 3     a[i] = 4
                                                 (Pointers and Arrays 1.1)
*p = 0       *p = 1       *p = 2       *p = 3       *p = 4
                                                 (Pointers and Arrays 1.2)

p[i] = 1     p[i] = 2     p[i] = 3     p[i] = 4     p[i] = ?
                                                 (Pointers and Arrays 1.3)
*(p+i) = 0   *(p+i) = 2   *(p+i) = 4             (Pointers and Arrays 1.4)

*p = 4       *p = 3       *p = 2       *p = 1       *p = 0
                                                 (Pointers and Arrays 1.5)
p[-i] = 4    p[-i] = 3    p[-i] = 2    p[-i] = 1   p[-i] = 0
                                                 (Pointers and Arrays 1.6)
a[p-a] = 4   a[p-a] = 3   a[p-a] = 2   a[p-a] = 1  a[p-a] = 0
                                                 (Pointers and Arrays 1.7)
```

Derivations begin on page 133.

Pointers and Arrays 2: Array of Pointers

What does the following program print?

```
#include "defs.h"

int a[] = { 0, 1, 2, 3, 4 };
int *p[] = { a, a+1, a+2, a+3, a+4 };
int **pp = p;                               (Pointers and Arrays 2.1)

main()
{
    PRINT2(d,a,*a);
    PRINT3(d,p,*p,**p);
    PRINT3(d,pp,*pp,**pp);                   (Pointers and Arrays 2.2)
    NL;

    pp++; PRINT3(d,pp-p,*pp-a,**pp);
    *pp++; PRINT3(d,pp-p,*pp-a,**pp);
    *++pp; PRINT3(d,pp-p,*pp-a,**pp);
    ++*pp; PRINT3(d,pp-p,*pp-a,**pp);        (Pointers and Arrays 2.3)
    NL;

    pp=p;
    **pp++; PRINT3(d,pp-p,*pp-a,**pp);
    *++*pp; PRINT3(d,pp-p,*pp-a,**pp);
    ++**pp; PRINT3(d,pp-p,*pp-a,**pp);       (Pointers and Arrays 2.4)
}
```

Pointers and Arrays 2: Array of Pointers

OUTPUT

a = address of a	*a = 0		*(Pointers and Arrays 2.2)*
p = address of p	*p = address of a	**p = 0	
pp = address of p	*pp = address of a	**pp = 0	

pp−p = 1	*pp−a = 1	**pp = 1	*(Pointers and Arrays 2.3)*
pp−p = 2	*pp−a = 2	**pp = 2	
pp−p = 3	*pp−a = 3	**pp = 3	
pp−p = 3	*pp−a = 4	**pp = 4	

pp−p = 1	*pp−a = 1	**pp = 1	*(Pointers and Arrays 2.4)*
pp−p = 1	*pp−a = 2	**pp = 2	
pp−p = 1	*pp−a = 2	**pp = 3	

Derivations begin on page 136.

Pointers and Arrays 3: Multidimensional Array

What does the following program print?

```
#include "defs.h"

int a[3][3] = {
    { 1, 2, 3 },
    { 4, 5, 6 },
    { 7, 8, 9 }
};
int *pa[3] = { a[0], a[1], a[2] };
int *p = a[0];                              (Pointers and Arrays 3.1)

main()
{
    int i;

    for( i=0; i<3; i++ )
        PRINT3(d, a[i][2-i], *a[i], *(*(a+i)+i) );
    NL;                                     (Pointers and Arrays 3.2)

    for( i=0; i<3; i++ )
        PRINT2(d, *pa[i], p[i] );           (Pointers and Arrays 3.3)
}
```

Pointers and Arrays 3: Multidimensional Array

OUTPUT

(Pointers and Arrays 3.2)

```
a[i][2-i] = 3      *a[i] = 1      *(*(a+i)+i) = 1
a[i][2-i] = 5      *a[i] = 4      *(*(a+i)+i) = 5
a[i][2-i] = 7      *a[i] = 7      *(*(a+i)+i) = 9
```

(Pointers and Arrays 3.3)

```
*pa[i] = 1      p[i] = 1
*pa[i] = 4      p[i] = 2
*pa[i] = 7      p[i] = 3
```

Derivations begin on page 140.

Pointers and Arrays 4: Pointer Stew

What does the following program print?

```
#include "defs.h"

char *c[] = {
    "ENTER",
    "NEW",
    "POINT",
    "FIRST"
};
char **cp[] = { c+3, c+2, c+1, c };
char ***cpp = cp;                              (Pointers and Arrays 4.1)

main()
{
    printf("%s", **++cpp );
    printf("%s ", *--*++cpp+3 );
    printf("%s", *cpp[-2]+3 );
    printf("%s\n", cpp[-1][-1]+1 );            (Pointers and Arrays 4.2)
}
```

Pointers and Arrays 4: Pointer Stew

OUTPUT

POINTER STEW   *(Pointers and Arrays 4.2)*

Derivation begins on page 142.

Structures

1. Simple Structure, Nested Structure

2. Array of Structures

3. Array of Pointers to Structures

A structure, that is, the C data type `struct`, is the fundamental building block for data structures. It provides a convenient way to package related data items.

Structures 1: Simple Structure, Nested Structure

What does the following program print?

```
#include "defs.h"

main()
{
    static struct S1 {
        char c[4], *s;
    } s1 = { "abc", "def" };
    static struct S2 {
        char *cp;
        struct S1 ss1;
    } s2 = { "ghi", { "jkl", "mno" } };            (Structures 1.1)

    PRINT2(c, s1.c[0], *s1.s);                      (Structures 1.2)
    PRINT2(s, s1.c, s1.s);                          (Structures 1.3)

    PRINT2(s, s2.cp, s2.ss1.s);                     (Structures 1.4)
    PRINT2(s, ++s2.cp, ++s2.ss1.s);                 (Structures 1.5)
}
```

Structures 1: Simple Structure, Nested Structure

OUTPUT

s1.c[0] = a	*s1.s = d	*(Structures 1.2)*
s1.c = abc	s1.s = def	*(Structures 1.3)*
s2.cp = ghi	s2.ss1.s = mno	*(Structures 1.4)*
++s2.cp = hi	++s2.ss1.s = no	*(Structures 1.5)*

Derivations begin on page 145.

Structures 2: Array of Structures

What does the following program print?

```
#include "defs.h"

struct S1 {
    char *s;
    int i;
    struct S1 *s1p;
};

main()
{
    static struct S1 a[] = {
        { "abcd", 1, a+1 },
        { "efgh", 2, a+2 },
        { "ijkl", 3, a }
    };
    struct S1 *p = a;                              (Structures 2.1)
    int i;

    PRINT3(s, a[0].s, p->s, a[2].s1p->s);          (Structures 2.2)

    for( i=0; i<2; i++ ) {
        PR(d, --a[i].i);
        PR(c, ++a[i].s[3]);                        (Structures 2.3)
        NL;
    }

    PRINT3(s, ++(p->s), a[(++p)->i].s, a[--(p->s1p->i)].s);
                                                   (Structures 2.4)

}
```

Structures 2: Array of Structures

OUTPUT

```
a[0].s = abcd    p->s = abcd    a[2].s1p->s = abcd   (Structures 2.2)
--a[i].i = 0     ++a[i].s[3] = e                      (Structures 2.3)
--a[i].i = 1     ++a[i].s[3] = i
++(p->s) = bce   a[(++p)->i].s = efgi   a[--(p->s1p->i)].s = ijkl
                                                      (Structures 2.4)
```

Derivations begin on page 149.

Structures 3: Array of Pointers to Structures

What does the following program print?

```
#include "defs.h"

struct S1 {
    char *s;
    struct S1 *s1p;
};

main()
{
    static struct S1 a[] = {
        { "abcd", a+1 },
        { "efgh", a+2 },
        { "ijkl", a }
    };
    struct S1 *p[3];                                    (Structures 3.1)
    int i;

    for( i=0; i<3; i++ ) p[i] = a[i].s1p;
    PRINT3(s, p[0]->s, (*p)->s, (**p).s);              (Structures 3.2)

    swap(*p,a);
    PRINT3(s, p[0]->s, (*p)->s, (*p)->s1p->s);         (Structures 3.3)

    swap(p[0], p[0]->s1p);
    PRINT3(s, p[0]->s, (*++p[0]).s, ++(*++(*p)->s1p).s);
                                                       (Structures 3.4)
}

swap( struct S1 *p1, struct S1 *p2 )
{
    struct S1 temp;

    temp.s = p1->s;
    p1->s = p2->s;
    p2->s = temp.s;
}
```

Structures 3: Array of Pointers to Structures

OUTPUT

```
p[0]->s = efgh    (*p)->s = efgh    (**p).s = efgh
                                          (Structures 3.2)
p[0]->s = abcd    (*p)->s = abcd    (*p)->slp->s = ijkl
                                          (Structures 3.3)
p[0]->s = ijkl    (*++p[0]).s = abcd ++(*++(*p)->slp).s = jkl
                                          (Structures 3.4)
```

Derivations begin on page 156.

Preprocessor

1. The Preprocessor Knows Little C

2. Caution Pays

Although in a strict sense the preprocessor is not part of the C language, few C programs would compile without it. Its two most important functions are macro substitution and file inclusion.

This section concentrates on macro substitution. When used judiciously, macros are a versatile tool that can enhance the readability and efficiency of a program. When used unwisely, macros, like other features in C, can lead to insidious bugs. To solve the puzzles in this section, follow the rules for expanding macros *very* carefully.

Preprocessor 1: The Preprocessor Knows Little C

What does the following program print?

```
#include <stdio.h>
#define FUDGE(k)        k+3.14159
#define PR(a)           printf(#a " = %d\t",(int)(a))
#define PRINT(a)        PR(a); putchar('\n')
#define PRINT2(a,b)     PR(a); PRINT(b)
#define PRINT3(a,b,c)   PR(a); PRINT2(b,c)
#define MAX(a,b)        (a<b ? b : a)

main()
{

    {
        int x=2;
        PRINT( x*FUDGE(2) );                    (Preprocessor 1.1)
    }


    {
        int cel;
        for( cel=0; cel<=100; cel+=50 )
            PRINT2( cel, 9./5*cel+32 );         (Preprocessor 1.2)
    }


    {
        int x=1, y=2;
        PRINT3( MAX(x++,y),x,y );
        PRINT3( MAX(x++,y),x,y );               (Preprocessor 1.3)
    }
}
```

Preprocessor 1: The Preprocessor Knows Little C

OUTPUT

```
x*2+3.14159 = 7                                          (Preprocessor 1.1)
cel = 0   cel = 50   cel = 100 9./5*cel+32 = 302  (Preprocessor 1.2)
(x++<y ? : x++) = 2      x = 2      y = 2            (Preprocessor 1.3)
(x++<y ? : x++) = 3      x = 4      y = 2
```

Derivations begin on page 162.

Preprocessor 2: Caution Pays

What does the following program print?

```
#include <stdio.h>
#define weeks(mins)    (days(mins)/7)
#define days(mins)     (hours(mins)/24)
#define hours(mins)    (mins/60)
#define mins(secs)     (secs/60)
#define PRINT(a)       printf(#a " = %d\n",(int)(a))
#define TRACE(x)       if(traceon) printf("Trace: "), PRINT(x)

#define g(a,b)         a a ## b(nd)
#define oo             "th"
#define oodbye(a)      "e e" # a

int traceon;

main()
{
    {
        PRINT( weeks(10080) );
        PRINT( days(mins(86400)) );          (Preprocessor 2.1)
    }


    {
        int i;
        traceon = 1;
        for( i=20; i>0; i/=2 ) {
            if( i<10 ) TRACE(i);
            else puts("not yet");            (Preprocessor 2.2)
        }
    }


    {
        puts( g(oo,dbye) );                  (Preprocessor 2.3)
    }
}
```

Preprocessor 2: Caution Pays

OUTPUT

```
weeks(10080) = 1
days(mins(86400)) = 1
Trace: i = 5
Trace: i = 2
Trace: i = 1
the end
```

(Preprocessor 2.1)

(Preprocessor 2.2)

(Preprocessor 2.3)

Derivations begin on page 165.

SOLUTIONS

Operators 1.1

`x = - 3 + 4 * 5 - 6`	Begin by reading the precedence table in Appendix 1 from top to bottom.
`x = (-3) + 4 * 5 - 6`	The highest level operator in the expression is the unary −. We'll use parentheses to indicate the order of binding operands to operators.
`x = (-3) + (4*5) - 6`	Next highest in the expression is *.
`x = ((-3)+(4*5)) - 6`	Both + and − are at the same precedence level. The order of binding thus depends on the associativity rule for that level. For + and −, associativity is left to right. First the + is bound.
`x = (((-3)+(4*5))-6)`	And then the −.
`(x=(((-3)+(4*5))-6))`	And finally, near the bottom of the precedence table is = . Now that we have completely identified the operands for each operator, we can evaluate the expression.
`(x=((-3+(4*5))-6))`	For this expression, evaluation proceeds from the inside out.
`(x=((-3+20)-6))`	Replace each subexpression by its value.
`(x=(17-6))`	
`(x=11)`	
`11, an integer`	The value of an assignment expression is the value of the right-hand side cast in the type of the left-hand side.

About printf. `Printf` is the formatted print routine that comes as part of the standard C library. The first argument to `printf` is a format string. It describes how any remaining arguments are to be printed. The character % begins a print specification for an argument. In our program, %d told `printf` to interpret and print the next argument as a decimal integer. `Printf` will also output literal characters. In our program, we "printed" a newline character by giving its name (\n) in the format string.

Operators 1.2

```
x = 3 + 4 % 5 - 6
```
This expression is very similar to the previous one.

```
x = 3 + (4%5) - 6
```
Following precedence

```
x = (3+(4%5)) - 6
```
and associativity

```
x = ((3+(4%5))-6)
```
leads to

```
(x=((3+(4%5))-6))
```
this. (The modulo, %, operator yields the remainder of dividing 4 by 5 .)

```
(x=((3+4)-6))
```
Again, evaluation is from the inside out.

```
(x=(7-6))
```

```
(x=1)
```

```
1
```


Operators 1.3

```
x = - 3 * 4 % - 6 / 5
```
This expression is a bit more complex than the last, but rigorous adherence to precedence and associativity will untangle it.

```
x = (-3) * 4 % (-6) / 5
```

```
x = ((-3)*4) % (-6) / 5
```
*, %, and / are all at the same precedence level, and they associate from left to right.

```
x = (((-3)*4)%(-6)) / 5
```

```
x = ((((-3)*4)%(-6))/5)
```

```
(x=((((-3)*4)%(-6))/5))
```

```
(x=(((-3*4)%-6)/5))
```
Evaluating from the inside out.

```
(x=((-12%-6)/5))
```

```
(x=(0/5))
```

```
(x=0)
```

```
0
```

Operators 1.4

`x = ( 7 + 6 ) % 5 / 2`	Of course we are not totally at the mercy of predefined precedence. Parentheses can always be used to effect or clarify a meaning.
`x = (7+6) % 5 / 2`	Subexpressions within parentheses bind first.
`x = ((7+6)%5) / 2`	Then, it is according to the precedence and associativity rules as before.
`x = (((7+6)%5)/2)`	
`(x=(((7+6)%5)/2))`	
`(x=((13%5)/2))`	Evaluating.
`(x=(3/2))`	
`(x=1)`	Integer arithmetic truncates any fractional part.

`1`

About programming style. As mentioned in the Preface, the programs in this book are not models to be copied. They were designed to make you think about the mechanics of how C works. But the puzzles do contain messages about program style. If a construct always forces you to consult a reference to find out how some detail is handled, then the construct is either not well written or it should be accompanied by a comment that provides the missing details.

The message from this first set of puzzles is to use parentheses in complex expressions to help the reader associate operands with operators.

Operators 2.1

initially x=2

x *= 3 + 2	Follow the precedence table.
x *= (3+2)	As we saw earlier, the assignment operators have precedence below the arithmetic operators. (*= is an assignment operator.)
(x*=(3+2))	
(x*=5)	Evaluating.
(x = x*5)	Expanding the assignment to its equivalent form.
(x=10)	
10	

About define. This program begins with the line

```
#define PRINTX printf("%d\n",x)
```

Any line in a C program that begins with the character # is a statement to the C Preprocessor. One job done by the Preprocessor is the substitution of one token string by another. The define statement in this program tells the Preprocessor to replace all instances of the token PRINTX with the string printf("%d\n",x).

Operators 2.2

initially x=10

x *= y = z = 4

x *= y = (z=4)   In this expression all the operators are
                                  assignments, hence associativity determines
                                  the order of binding. Assignment operators
                                  associate from right to left.

x *= (y=(z=4))

(x*=(y=(z=4)))

(x*=(y=4))   Evaluating.

(x*=4)

40

Operators 2.3

initially y=4, z=4

x = y == z

x = (y==z)   Often a source of confusion for
                                  programmers new to C is the distinction
                                  between = (assignment) and == (test for
                                  equality). From the precedence table it can
                                  be seen that == is bound before =.

(x=(y==z))

(x=(TRUE))

(x=1)   Relational and equality operators yield a
                                  result of TRUE, an integer 1, or FALSE, an
                                  integer 0.

1

Operators 2.4

initially x=1, z=4

x == (y = z)

(x==(y=z))   In this expression the assignment has been forced to have higher precedence than the test for equality through the use of parentheses.

(x==4)   Evaluating.

FALSE, or 0   The value of the expression is 0. Note however that the value of x has not changed (== does not change its operands), so PRINTX prints 1.

Operators 3.1

```
initially x=2, y=1, z=0

x = x && y || z

x = (x&&y) || z                          Bind operands to operators according to
                                         precedence.

x = ((x&&y)||z)

(x=((x&&y)||z))

(x=((TRUE&&TRUE)||z))                     Logical operators are evaluated from left to
                                          right. An operand to a logical operator is
                                          FALSE if it is zero and TRUE if it is
                                          anything else.

(x=(TRUE||z))                             The logical AND, &&, yields TRUE only
                                          when both its operands are TRUE, otherwise
                                          FALSE.

(x=(TRUE||whatever))                      Once one argument to the logical OR, ||, is
                                          known to be TRUE we know the result of
                                          the || will be TRUE regardless of the other
                                          operand. Hence there is no need to evaluate
                                          the expression further.

(x=TRUE)

(x=1)

1
```

More about define. The define statement that begins this program is a little fancier than that in the previous program. Here, PRINT is the name of a *macro with arguments.* The Preprocessor performs two levels of substitution on macros with arguments: first the actual arguments are substituted for the formal arguments in the macro body, then the resulting macro body is substituted for the macro call.

In this program, PRINT has one formal argument, int. PRINT(x) is a call of PRINT with the actual argument x. To expand PRINT, each occurrence of int in the macro body is replaced by x, and then the resulting string, "printf("%d\n",x)", is substituted for the call, PRINT(x). Notice that the formal parameter int did not match the middle letters in printf. This is because the formal arguments of a macro are identifiers; int only matches the *identifier* int.

Operators 3.2

initially x=1, y=1, z=0

x || ! y && z

x || (!y) && z   Binding operands to operators.

x || ((!y)&&z)

(x||((!y)&&z))

(TRUE||((!y)&&z))   Evaluating from left to right.

(TRUE||whatever)

TRUE, or 1

Operators 3.3

initially x=1, y=1

z = x ++ - 1

z = (x++) - 1   Following precedence.

z = ((x++)-1)

(z=((x++)-1))

(z=(1-1)), and x=2   The ++ to the right of its operand is a post
                                        increment. This means that x is
                                        incremented after its value is used in the
                                        expression.

(z=0)

0

Operators 3.4

```
initially x=2, y=1, z=0

z += - x ++ + ++ y

z += - (x++) + (++y)
```

Unary operators associate from right to left, thus the ++ binds before the unary –. (Actually the expression would not be legal if it were arranged so that the – bound first since ++ and –– operators expect a variable (an *lvalue*) as their operand. x is an lvalue, but –x is not.)

```
z += (-(x++)) + (++y)

z += ((-(x++))+(++y))

(z+=((-(x++))+(++y)))

(z+=((-2)+2)), and x=3, y=2
```

Evaluating from the inside out.

```
(z+=0)

(z = 0+0)

(z=0)

0
```

About tokens. The text of a program can be thought of as a sequence of tokens. The first job in translating a program is to identify each of the tokens. Usually this is easy, but there are sequences that can be confusing. Suppose part of the example above had been written without spaces:

```
x+++++y
```

Is this expression equivalent to the expression with spaces?

To remove ambiguity, if a string can be interpreted as more than one operator, C always chooses the operator that consists of the most characters. Thus x+++++y is interpreted as

```
x++ ++ + y
```

which is not a valid expression.

Operators 3.5

```
initially x=3, z=0

z = x / ++ x

z = x / (++x)

z = (x/(++x))

(z=(x/(++x)))
```

You may be tempted at this point to begin evaluating this expression as before, from the inside out. First the value of x would be retrieved and incremented to be divided into the value of x. One question that might be asked is what value is retrieved from x for the numerator, 3 or 4? That is, is the value for the numerator retrieved before or after the increment is stored? The C language does not specify when such a side effect† actually occurs; that is left to the compiler writer. The message is to avoid writing expressions that depend upon knowing when a side effect will occur.

---

† A side effect is any change to the state of a program that occurs as a byproduct of executing a statement. The most common side effects in C relate to storing values in variables, such as with the increment operator as above or with an assignment operator.

Operators 4.1

initially `x=03, y=02, z=01`

`x	y & z`	Integer constants that begin with a 0 (zero) are octal values. Octal notation is useful when working with the bitwise operators because it is easy to translate octal numbers to binary. In this problem `01`, `02`, and `03` are equivalent to 1, 2, and 3 so using octal is merely a cue to the reader that the program will deal with the values of x, y, and z as bit strings.
`(x|(y&z))`	Following precedence.
`(x|(02&01))`	The innermost expression is evaluated first.
`(x|0)`	In binary, `01=1, 02=10, 03=11`

```
  10
& 01
____
  00.
```

`(03|0)`

`03`

```
  00
| 11
____
  11
```

The PRINT macro. The macro `PRINT` in this program uses the `#` operator of the Preprocessor and string concatenation. `PRINT` has a formal argument `int`. On expansion, `int` is replaced by the actual argument in the macro call. When a `#` precedes a formal argument, the actual argument is enclosed in double quotes. Thus

```
PRINT( x | y & z )
```

becomes

```
printf("x | y & z" " = %d\n",x | y & z)
```

Adjacent string literals are concatenated, so this is equivalent to

```
printf("x | y & z = %d\n",x | y & z)
```

Operators 4.2

initially `x=03, y=02, z=01`

`x | y & ~ z`

`(x|(y&(~z)))`

`(x|(y&~01))`

`~` complements each of the bits of its operand. Thus $0\ldots01$ becomes $1\ldots10$.

`(x|(02&~01))`

`(03|02)`

In binary,

```
   0...010
&  1...110
   ───────
   0000010.
```

3

```
   10
|  11
   ──
   11
```

Operators 4.3

initially `x=03, y=02, z=01`

`x ^ y & ~ z`

`(x^(y&(~z)))`

This is the same as the previous problem except that the exclusive OR, `^`, has been substituted for the inclusive OR, `|`.

`(x^(02&~01))`

`(03^02)`

1

In binary,

```
   10
^  11
   ──
   01.
```

Operators 4.4

initially `x=03, y=02, z=01`

`x & y && z`

`((x&y)&&z)`

`((03&02)&&z)`

`(02&&z)`

`(TRUE&&z)`

`(TRUE&&01)`

`(TRUE&&TRUE)`

`TRUE, or 1`   `&&` yields TRUE whenever both operands are TRUE.

Operators 4.5

initially `x=01`

`! x | x`

`((!x)|x)`

`((!TRUE)|x)`

`(FALSE|01)`

`(0|01)`

`01`

Operators 4.6

initially `x=01`

`~ x | x`

`((~x)|x)`

`(~01|01)`

`-1`

In binary,

```
   1...110
| 0...001
  _____
   1...111, or -1.
```

(The answer is the same for all values of x.
Actually it is −1 on a twos complement
machine, like the Intel 8086 and the
Motorola 68000. On a ones complement
machine 1...1 would be −0. For the few
cases in this book where it matters, twos
complement will be used.)

Operators 4.7

initially `x=01`

`x ^ x`

`(01^01)`

`0`

In binary,

```
   0...01
^ 0...01
  _____
   0...00.
```

(The answer is the same for all values of x.)

Operators 4.8

> initially `x=01`
>
> `x <<= 3`
>
> `x = 01<<3`
>
> `x=8`

In binary,

```
      0000...01
<<           3
```
———————
```
      0...01000, which is 8.
```

Each place shifted to the left is an effective multiplication by 2.

Operators 4.9

> initially `y=-01`
>
> `y <<= 3`
>
> `y = -01<<3`
>
> `y = -8`

In binary,

```
      1111...11
<<           3
```
———————
```
      1...11000, or -8.
```

Operators 4.10

> initially `y=-08`
>
> `y >>= 3`
>
> `y = -08>>3`

PRESUMPTION: WHEN YOU SHIFT A NEGATIVE # TO THE RIGHT, THE SIGN BIT PROPAGATES

It is tempting at this point to assume that y=-1. Unfortunately this is not always the case, since the computer may not preserve the sign of a number when shifting. C does not guarantee that the shift will be arithmetically correct. In any case, there is a much clearer way to divide by 8, namely y / 8.

Operators 5.1

initially `x=3, y=2, z=1`

`x < y ? y : x`

`(x<y) ? (y) : (x)`   The conditional operator, aside from it taking three operands, is parsed like any other operator.

`((x<y)?(y):(x))`

`(FALSE?(y):(x))`   First the condition is evaluated. Then either the true part or the false part is evaluated, but not both.

`((x))`   In this problem the value of the condition is FALSE, thus the value of the conditional expression is the value of the false part.

`(3)`

`3`

Operators 5.2

initially `x=3, y=2, z=1`

`x < y ? x ++ : y ++`

`((x<y)?(x++):(y++))`

`(FALSE?(x++):(y++))`   First evaluate the condition.

`((y++))`   The condition is FALSE so the false part is evaluated.

`(2), and y=3`

`2`   (And since x++ was not evaluated, x remains 3.)

Operators 5.3

```
initially x=3, y=3, z=1
z += x < y ? x ++ : y ++
(z+=((x<y)?(x++):(y++)))
(z+=(FALSE?(x++):(y++)))
(z+=((y++)))
```
The result of the conditional expression is the value of the right-hand side of the assignment.

```
(z+=(3)), and y=4
(z=z+3)
(z=4)
4
```

Operators 5.4

```
initially x=3, y=4, z=4
(z >= y >= x) ? 1 : 0
(((z>=y)>=x)?(1):(0))
((TRUE>=x)?(1):(0))
```
The condition is evaluated from the inside out.

```
((1>=x)?(1):(0))
```
The value of the innermost relation is TRUE. It is compared to the integer x. While this is legal in C, it is really playing footloose with the value TRUE being an integer 1, and, as in this problem, it is usually not what's wanted. (The next puzzle shows the right way to compare three values.)

```
(FALSE?(1):(0))
((0))
0
```

Operators 5.5

initially x=3, y=4, z=4

z >= y && y >= x

((z>=y)&&(y>=x))

(TRUE&&(y>=x))   Evaluating from left to right.

(TRUE&&TRUE)

(TRUE)

1

Operators 6.1

```
initially x=1, y=1, z=1

++ x || ++ y && ++ z

((++x) || ((++y) && (++z)))                 Binding operands to operators.

(2 || ((++y) && (++z))), and x=2            Evaluating from left to right.

(TRUE||whatever)                            Since the left operand of the || is
                                            TRUE, there is no need to evaluate
                                            further.  In fact, C guarantees that it
                                            will not evaluate further.  The rule is
                                            that a logical expression is evaluated
                                            from left to right until its truth value
                                            is known.  For this problem that
                                            means y and z remain 1.

TRUE, or 1
```

Operators 6.2

```
initially x=1, y=1, z=1

++ x && ++ y || ++ z

(((++x) && (++y)) || (++z))

((TRUE&&(++y)) || (++z)), and x=2

((2&&2) || (++z)), and x=2                  Evaluating from left to right.

(TRUE||(++z))

TRUE, or 1                                  z is not affected.
```

Operators 6.3

```
initially x=1, y=1, z=1

++ x && ++ y && ++ z

(((++x)&&(++y))&&(++z))

((2&&2)&&(++z)),  and x=2, y=2

(TRUE&&(++z))

(TRUE&&TRUE),  and z=2

TRUE,  or 1
```

Operators 6.4

```
initially x=-1, y=-1, z=-1

++ x && ++ y || ++ z

(((++x)&&(++y))||(++z))

((0&&(++y))||(++z)),  and x=0

((FALSE&&(++y))||(++z))

(FALSE||(++z))
```

There is no need to evaluate ++y since the left operand to && is FALSE. The value of the || is still not known yet, however.

```
(FALSE||(0)),  and z=0

(FALSE||FALSE)

FALSE,  or 0
```

Operators 6.5

```
initially x=-1,  y=-1,  z=-1

++ x || ++ y && ++ z

((++x)||((++y)&&(++z)))

(FALSE||((++y)&&(++z))), and x=0

(FALSE||(FALSE&&(++z))), and y=0

(FALSE||FALSE)

FALSE, or 0
```

Operators 6.6

```
initially x=-1,  y=-1,  z=-1

++ x && ++ y && ++ z

(((++x)&&(++y))&&(++z))

((FALSE&&(++y))&&(++z)), and x=0

(FALSE&&(++z))

FALSE, or 0
```

'C' LOGICAL AND'S AND OR'S
ARE SHORT-CIRCUIT AND'S AND
OR'S

About side effects in logical expressions. As you have surely learned by now, the evaluation of a logical expression can be tricky in C because the right-hand part of the expression is evaluated *conditionally* on the value of the left-hand part. Actually, conditional evaluation is a useful property of the logical operators. The trouble arises when the right-hand part of a logical expression contains a side effect; sometimes the side effect will occur and sometimes it won't. So, while in general it is good practice to use side effects cautiously, in logical expressions it is vital.

Basic Types 1.1

PRINT(d, "5")	%d format instructs printf to print the argument as a decimal number. "5" is a pointer to a character array (i.e., the address of the two character array '5', ' ').
PRINT(d, '5')	%d causes the decimal value of the character '5' to be printed.†
PRINT(d, 5)	The integer 5 is printed in decimal.
PRINT(s, "5")	%s format instructs printf that the argument is a string, i.e., a pointer to a character array. Since "5" is a pointer to a character array, the content of that array, 5, is printed.
PRINT(c, '5')	%c format instructs printf to translate the argument into the character its value represents. Since '5' is the encoded value for 5, 5 is printed.
PRINT(c, 53)	As seen earlier, the decimal number 53 is the ASCII code value for the character 5.
PRINT(d, ('5'>5))	One last time. '5' has the integer value 53 which is greater than the integer 5.

---

† The value given here is that for the ASCII character code (see Appendix 3). The ASCII code is but one of several codes used by computers to represent characters. It will be used in this book for those few cases where it matters.

Basic Types 1.2

initially `x=-2, ux=-2`

x is signed, `ux` is unsigned.

`PRINT(o,x)`

i,e, sign bit is not taken into account for printing purposes

`%o` instructs `printf` to print the argument as an octal number. In the two complement representation of octal the highest order bit of a negative number is 1. On a computer with 16-bit integers (such as the Intel 8086) this means that the leftmost octal digit is a 1.

`PRINT(o,ux)`

−2 is a string of 1's and 0's just as valid for unsigned variables as for signed ones.

`PRINT(d,x/2)`

For signed variables, division of negative numbers works as expected.

`PRINT(d,ux/2)`

For unsigned variables, negative numbers are interpreted as large positive values.

`PRINT(o,x>>1)`

We have seen this problem earlier. With some versions of C, right shifting of a signed integer causes the sign bit to be copied into the vacated high order bits, thus having the desirable property of preserving sign. *Beware, this is compiler dependent!*

`PRINT(o,ux>>1)`

When right shifting an unsigned integer the high order bits are always filled with 0's.

`PRINT(d,x>>1)`

In decimal, right shifting a signed −2 one place yields the expected −1 if sign is preserved, 32767 otherwise (in twos complement on a 16-bit machine).

`PRINT(d,ux>>1)`

For an unsigned −2, the result is always 32767.

Basic Types 2.1

```
i = 1 = f = d = 100/3
```

```
i= (l= (f= (d= (100/3)) )))
```
Evaluation is from right to left.

```
i= (l= (f= (d=33) )))
```
Since both 100 and 3 are integers, the division is integer division and thus the quotient is truncated.

```
i= (l= (f=(double)33) )), and d=33
```
Recall that the value of an assignment expression is the value of the right-hand side cast in the type of the left-hand side.

```
i= (l=(float)33) ), and f=33
```

```
i=(long)33), and l=33
```

```
(int)33), and i=33
```

```
33, an int
```

Basic Types 2.2

```
d = f = l = i = 100/3
```

```
(d= (f= (l= (i=(100/3)) )))
```

```
(d= (f= (l=(int)33) )), and i=33
```

```
(d= (f=(long)33) ), and l=33
```

```
(d=(float)33), and f=33
```

```
((double)33), and d=33
```

```
33, a double
```

Basic Types 2.3

```
i = l = f = d = 100/3.

i= (l= (f= (d= (100/3.)) )))

i= (l= (f=(double)33.333333) ))
```

        and d=33.333333

> 3. is a double so the quotient retains its precision.

```
i= (l=(float)33.333333) )
```

        and f=33.33333x

> The printf specification in this program is %.8g, which tells printf to output up to eight significant digits. Seven significant digits is the limit of precision for floats on the Intel 8086 and Motorola 68000, so the eighth digit is unreliable.

```
i=(long)33.33333x), and l=33
```

> The float to long conversion is through truncation.

```
(int)33), and i=33

33, an int
```

Basic Types 2.4

```
d = f = l = i = (double)100/3

(d= (f= (l= (i= ((double)100)/3))))
```

> Note that type cast has higher precedence than /.

```
(d= (f= (l= (i=33.333333) )))

(d= (f= (l=(int)33.333333) )), and i=33

(d= (f=(long)33) ), and l=33

(d=(float)33), and f=33

((double)33), and d=33

33, a double
```

Basic Types 2.5

```
i = l = f = d = (double)(100000/3)

(i= (l= (f= (d= ((double)(100000/3)) ))))

(i= (l= (f= (d=(double)33333) )))
```

The operand to the type cast is the quotient from the integer division of 100000 by 3.

```
(i= (l= (f=(double)33333) )),

        and d=33333

(i= (l=(float)33333) ), and f=33333

(i=(long)33333), and l=33333

((int)33333), and i=33333 or overflow
```

33333 cannot be represented as a 16-bit signed integer. Most implementations of C will happily permit arithmetic over- or underflow. When your calculations push the limits of your machine, it is wise to insert explicit range checks.

```
33333, an int, or overflow
```

Basic Types 2.6

```
d = f = l = i = 100000/3

(d= (f= (l= (i=100000/3) )))

(d= (f= (l=(int)33333) ))
```

        and i=overflow

As we've seen before, 33333 is overflow for a 16-bit signed integer. For larger integer sizes i would get 33333, as would l, f, and d.

```
(d= (f=(long)-32203) )
```

        and l=-32203

The result of an operation that leads to overflow is a legitimate number, just not the number expected. The 33333 is lost, regardless of future type casts.

```
(d=(float)-32203), and f=-32203

((double)-32203), and d=-32203

-32203, a double
```

About numbers. The treatment of numbers is not one of C's strong points. C does not provide a way to catch arithmetic errors even if the hardware so obliges. The range of the numerical data types is fixed by the compiler writer; there is no way to specify a range in the language. To achieve range checking, about the best one can do is test the value of variables explicitly at critical points in a calculation.

Basic Types 3.1

```
initially d=3.2, i=2
x = (y=d/i)*2
(x= (y=3.2/2) *2)
(x= (y=1.6)*2)
```
3.2, a double, is of higher type than 2, an int. Thus, the quotient is a double.

```
(x=1*2), and y=1
```
y, an int, gets 1.6 truncated.

```
(x=2)
2, and x=2
```

Basic Types 3.2

```
initially d=3.2, i=2
y = (x=d/i)*2
(y= (x=1.6)*2)
(y=1.6*2), and x=1.6
```
Since x is a double, the result of the assignment is a double.

```
(y=3.2)
```
1.6, a double,

```
3, and y=3
```
y, an int, gets 3.2 truncated.

Basic Types 3.3

    initially `d=3.2, i=2`

    `y = d * (x=2.5/d)`

    `(y= d* (x=2.5/d) )`

    `(y= d*2.5/d ), and x=2.5/d`   x is a `double`, so the precision of `2.5/d` is retained.

    `(y=2.5)`

    `2, and y=2`   y gets `2.5` truncated.

Basic Types 3.4

    initially `d=3.2, i=2`

    `x = d * (y = ((int)2.9+1.1)/d)`

    `(x= d* (y=(2+1.1)/d) )`   Type cast has higher precedence than +.

    `(x= d* (y=3.1/d) )`

    `(x= d* (y=.something) )`

    `(x=d*0), and y=0`   y gets 0 regardless of the value of "something", since ".something" is between 0 and 1.

    `0, and x=0`

About mixing types. By now you have seen enough examples of how mixing floating point and integer values in expressions can lead to surprises. It is best to avoid arithmetic with operands of mixed type. If you do need it, make the type conversions explicit by *carefully* using casts.

Control Flow 1.1

    initially `y=1`

    `if( y!=0 ) x=5`   The first step is to evaluate the condition.

    `( y!=0 )`

    `( 1!=0 )`

    `TRUE`   Since the condition is TRUE, the true part of the `if` statement is executed.

    `x = 5`

Control Flow 1.2

    initially `y=1`

    `if( y==0 ) x=3; else x=5`

    `( y==0 )`   Evaluate the condition.

    `FALSE`

    `x = 5`   Executing the false part of the `if` statement.

Control Flow 1.3

    initially `y=1`

    `x=1`

    `if( y<0 ) if( y>0 ) x=3;`

    `else x=5;`

    `x=1`   First x is assigned 1.

    `( y<0 )`

    `FALSE`   The condition of the first `if` is FALSE, thus the true part is skipped. The `else` clause is contained in the true part of the first `if` since it belongs to the second `if`. The rule in C is that an `else` clause belongs to the closest `if` that can accept it.

AN ELSE BELONG

Control Flow 1.4

```
initially y=1
if( z=y<0 ) x=3
else if( y==0 ) x=5
else x = 7
```

`( z=(y<0) )`	Begin by evaluating the first condition. We will use parentheses, as before, to indicate the binding of operands to operators.

`( z=(1<0) )`
`( z=FALSE )`
`FALSE, and z=0`
`( y==0 )`
	Since the condition of the first `if` statement is FALSE, the false part of the `if` is executed. It is another `if` statement, so its condition is evaluated.

`FALSE` `x = 7`	The condition is FALSE, thus the false part of the second `if` statement is executed.

Control Flow 1.5

initially `y=1`	
`if( z=(y==0) ) x=5; x=3`	
`if( z=(y==0) ) x=5;`	The true part of an `if` is the single statement or block following the condition for the `if`.
`( z=(y==0) )`	Evaluate the condition.
`( z=FALSE )`	
`FALSE, and z = 0`	
`x = 3`	Since the `if` statement does not have a false part, control falls through to the next statement.

Control Flow 1.6

initially `y=1`	
`if( x=z=y ); x=3`	
`if( x=z=y );`	The true part of the `if` is a null statement.
`( x=(z=y)) )`	Evaluate the condition.
`( x=(z=1))`	
`( x=1 ), and z = 1`	
`TRUE, and x=1`	
`x = 3`	The `if` condition is TRUE, so the true part of the `if` is executed. The true part is a null statement that has no effect. Finally, the statement following the `if` is executed.

Control Flow 2.1

initially `x=0, y=0`

`while( y<10 ) ++y; x += y`	Begin by analyzing the factors that control the execution of the `while` statement:
`( y<10 )`	The *loop condition*. The body of the loop is executed as long as the loop condition evaluates to TRUE.
`( y>=10 )`	The *exit condition*. The exit condition, the negation of the loop condition, is TRUE upon a normal termination of the loop.
`y=0`	The *initial value* of the control variable. This is the value of the control variable at the start of the first iteration of the loop body.
`++y`	The *effect* on the control variable of executing the body of the loop.
`y = 0  through  9  in the loop`	`y=0` the first time in the loop. Each time through the body `y` is incremented by 1.
`y = 10  on exit`	When `y=10` the loop condition evaluates to FALSE and the iteration terminates.
`x += y`	Control passes to the statement following the loop body.
`x = 0+10`	
`x = 10`	

Control Flow 2.2

initially `x=0, y=0`

`while( y<10 ) x += ++y`

`( y<10 )`	The loop condition.
`( y>=10 )`	The exit condition.
`y=0`	The initial value of the control variable.
`++y`	The effect of the loop on the control variable.
`y = 0 through 9` in the loop	As in the previous problem.
`x += ++y`	x gets the sum of the values of y (after y is incremented) in the loop.
`x = 55`	The sum of the integers 1 to 10.
`y = 10` on exit	

Control Flow 2.3

initially `y=1`

`while( y<10 ) { x = y++; z = ++y; }`

`( y<10 )`	The loop condition.
`( y>=10 )`	The exit condition.
`y=1`	The initial value of the control variable.
`y++, ++y`	The effect of the loop on the control variable.
`y = 1,3,5,7,9` in the loop	y=1 the first time in the loop and is incremented by 2 each time through the loop.
`x = 1,3,5,7,9`	x takes on the value of y in the loop before it is incremented.
`z = 3,5,7,9,11`	z takes on the value of y in the loop after it has been incremented by 2.
`y = 11` on exit	

Control Flow 2.4

```
for( y=1; y<10; y++ ) x=y
```
The `for` statement aggregates the controlling factors of the loop.

`y<10`	Loop condition.
`y>=10`	Exit condition.
`y=1`	Initial value.
`y++`	Effect.
`y = 1 through 9 in the loop`	
`x = 1 through 9`	x gets the value of y in the body of the loop.
`y = 10 on exit`	

Control Flow 2.5

```
for( y=1; (x=y)<10; y++ ) ;
```

`y<10`	Loop condition.
`y>=10`	Exit condition.
`y=1`	Initial value.
`y++`	Effect.
`y = 1 through 9 in the loop`	
`x = 1 through 10`	x gets the value of y just before the evaluation of the loop condition. Notice that the condition is evaluated one time more than the body is executed.
`y = 10 on exit`	

Control Flow 2.6

```
for( x=0,y=1000; y>1; x++,y/=10 )
        PRINT2 (d,x,y)
```

y>1   Loop condition.

y<=1   Exit condition.

y=1000   Initial value.

y/=10   Effect.

y = 1000,100,10 in the loop

x = 0,1,2 in the loop   x=0 from the for statement
                                            initialization. x is incremented
                                            after the body and *before* the test.
                                            (The PRINT2 statement is in the
                                            body.)

y = 1 on exit

x = 3 on exit

Control Flow 3.1

initially `i=in=high=low=0`, `input="PI=3.14159, approximately"`

`while( c=(NEXT(i)!=EOS) )`	The loop condition effectively is `NEXT(i)!=EOS`, where `NEXT(i)` successively takes on the character values from `input`. `c` gets the truth value of `NEXT(i)!=EOS`, which, by definition, is `TRUE` in the loop and `FALSE` on exit.
`if( 1<'0' ) low++`	`c` is always 1 in the loop, so `low` is always incremented (1 < 060).
`while( c=(I!=EOS) )`	On the second pass, `next(i)=I`. The iteration continues until all the characters in `input` have been read. C uses the ASCII `nul` character, 0, as the end-of-string marker.

Control Flow 3.3

initially `done=i=in=high=low=0`, `input="PI=3.14159, approximately"`	
`while( (c=NEXT(i))!=EOS && !done ) {`	c successively takes on the value of each character from `input`.
`if( 'P'<'0' )`	FALSE.
`else if( 'P'>'9' )`	TRUE.
`++high<ENUF ?`	`high`, after being incremented is not equal to ENUF, so `done` is assigned FALSE. `high=1`.
`while( 'I'!=EOS && !done )`	TRUE.
`if( 'I'<'0' )`	FALSE.
`else if( 'I'>'9' )`	TRUE.
`done = (++high==ENUF)`	`high=2`, `done=FALSE`.
`while( '='!=EOS && !done )`	TRUE.
`if( '='<'0' )`	FALSE.
`else if( '='>'9' )`	TRUE.
`done = (++high==ENUF)`	`high=3`, `done=TRUE`.
`while( '3'!=EOS && !done )`	`done==TRUE` so `!done=FALSE` is true, and the loop terminates.

Control Flow 4.1

```
char input[]="SSSWILTECH1\1\11W\1WALLMP1"
```
The character array input is initialized to the character string "SSS...MP1".

```
for(i=2; (c=input[2])!='\0';
```
c takes character values from input beginning at the third character.

```
switch('S') {
```
The first time through the switch statement c='S'.

```
default: putchar('S')
```
The default case is taken since none of the cases match 'S'. S is printed.

```
continue
```
The continue statement forces the next iteration of the innermost enclosing loop; in this case, the for loop. Notice that continue effectively is a branch to the reinitialization expression of the for.

```
for( ;(c=input[3])!='\0'; i++) {
```
c gets the fourth character from input.

```
switch('W') {
```
c='W'.

```
default: putchar('W'); continue
```
As before; W is printed.

```
    ...
```
Similarly for i=4, c='I'.

```
switch('L') {
```
i=5, c='L'.

```
case 'L': continue
```
The 'L' case is taken; nothing is printed.

```
  i=5, c='L';
```
Nothing is printed.

```
  i=6, c='T';
```
T is printed.

```
  i=7, c='E';
```
Nothing is printed.

`i=8, c='C';`	C is printed.
`i=9, c='H';`	H is printed.
`switch('1') {`	i=10, c='1'.
`case '1': break`	The `break` statement forces an exit from the innermost enclosing loop or `switch`. In this case it effects a branch to the statement following the end of the `switch`.
`putchar(' ')`	A space is printed.
`for( ; (c=input[11])!='\0'; i++) {`	Back to the top of the `for` loop.
`switch('\1') {`	The character constant `'\n'`, where n is up to three octal digits, yields a character with the octal value n. For instance, `\0` yields the ASCII character `nul`, and `\101` the character A.
`case 1:`	Case labels may be either character or integer constants. `\1` matches the integer 1 since C automatically coerces `char` to `int`.
`while( (c=input[++i])!='\1' || c=='\0') ;`	The exit condition for the `while` is either `c=='\1'` or end of string. Each time the `while` test is made, i is incremented by 1, thus the loop advances i past the characters of `input` until either the next `'\1'` character or the end of string.

In the while loop:

`i=12, c='\11';`	Nothing is printed.
`i=13, c='W';`	Nothing is printed.
`i=14, c='\1';`	The `while` loop terminates.

`case 9: putchar('S')`	The statements from each case follow one another directly; there is no implied `break` between cases. Case 9 follows case 1. S is printed.
`case 'E': case 'L': continue`	Cases `'E'` and `'L'` follow case 9.
`for( ; (c=input[15]); i++) {`	Again, back to the top of the `for` loop.

In the for loop:

`i=15, c='W';`	W is printed.
`i=16, c='A';`	A is printed.
`i=17, c='L';`	Nothing is printed.
`i=18, c='L';`	Nothing is printed.
`i=19, c='M';`	M is printed.
`i=20, c='P';`	P is printed.
`i=21, c='1';`	A space is printed.
`i=22, c='\0';`	The `for` loop terminates.

`putchar('\n')`

Programming Style 1.1

The need for a `continue` statement can often be satisfied by altering a test condition. The resulting code is sometimes remarkably cleaner.

For this problem simply negating the test to the `if` statement will do.

```
while(A)
    if(!B) C;
```

Programming Style 1.2

The `do...while` is another of the C constructs that can sometimes be replaced to advantage. If either a `do...while` or a `while` can be used, the `while` is always preferred.

In this problem the `if` and `do...while` are redundant, they are effecting a `while`.

```
do {                          First eliminate the continue.
    if(A) { B; C; }
} while(A);
```

```
while(A) {                    Then replace the do...while and if with a while.
    B; C;
}
```

Programming Style 1.3

The problem of deeply nested `if` statements is well known to experienced programmers: by the time one gets to the innermost condition, the surrounding conditions have been forgotten or obscured. The counter approach is to qualify each condition fully, but this tends to generate long conditions that are obscure from the start. Alas, good judgement must prevail!

Here are two possibilities for this problem. The first shows the full condition for each case:

```
if( A && B && C ) D;
else if( !A && B && C ) E;
else if( !A && B && !C ) F;
```

The second is more trouble to read, but more efficient to execute:

```
if( B ) {
    if( A ) {
        if( C ) D;
    } else {
        if( C ) E;
        else F;
    }
}
```

Programming Style 1.4

This problem has a straightforward idea hierarchy:

- while there are more characters on the line
    - multiway switch based on character type
        - return ALPHA
        - return DIGIT
        - return OTHER.

This translates easily into C:

```
while( (c=getchar()) != '\n' ) {
    if( c>='a' && c<='z' ) return ALPHA;
    else if( c>='0' && c<='9' ) return DIGIT;
    else if( c!=' ' && c!='\t' ) return OTHER;
}
return(EOL);
```

Programming Style 2.1

```
done = i = 0;
while( i<MAXI && !DONE ) {
    if( (x/=2) > 1 ) i++;
    else done++;
}
```

The first observation is that the `if...continue` construct is effecting an `if...else`. So make it an `if...else`!

```
i = 0;
while( i<MAXI && (x/=2)>1 ) i++;
```

Then it becomes clear that
- one loop condition is done equal to FALSE;
- done is FALSE as long as the `if` condition is TRUE;
- thus, one loop condition is $(x/2)>1$.

Make it explicit!

```
for( i=0; i<MAXI && (x/=2)>1; i++ ) ;
```

A `while` statement that is preceded by an initialization and that contains a change of the loop control variable is exactly a `for` statement.

Programming Style 2.2

There are usually many ways to express an idea in C. A useful guideline is to group ideas into chunks. C provides a hierarchy of packaging for these chunks:

- the lowest level ideas become expressions;
- expressions are grouped together into statements;
- statements are grouped together into blocks and functions.

In this problem there is a two level idea hierarchy. At the lowest level are the expressions B, D, F, and G. They are related as the mutually exclusive cases of a multiway switch. A cohesive representation for a general multiway switch is the `if...else if` construction:

```
if(A) B;
else if(C) D;
else if(E) F;
else G;
return;
```

Programming Style 2.3

The key observation in this problem is that the underlying structure is a three-way switch with mutually exclusive cases.

```
plusflg = zeroflg = negflg = 0;

if( a>0 ) ++plusflg;
else if( a==0 ) ++zeroflg;
else ++negflg;
```

Programming Style 2.4

```
i = 0;
while( (c=getchar())!=EOF && c!='\n' ) {
    if( c!='\n' && c!='\t' ) {
        s[i++] = c;
        continue;
    }
    if( c=='\t' ) c = ' ';
    s[i++] = c;
}
```

Reformatting the statements to indicate nesting is a good start. Then look closer at the break and continue statements to see if they are really necessary. The break goes easily by adding the negation of the break condition to the condition for the while.

```
i = 0;
while( (c=getchar())!=EOF && c!='\n' ) {
    if( c!='\t' ) {
        s[i++] = c;
        continue;
    }
    if( c=='\t' ) s[i++] = ' ';
}
```

The first if condition can then be reduced. (c!='\n' is now a loop condition, hence it must always be TRUE in the if test.)

```
i = 0;
while( (c=getchar())!=EOF && c!='\n' )
    if( c!='\t' ) s[i++] = c;
    else s[i++] = ' ';
```

The continue statement is effecting an if...else.

```
for( i=0; (c=getchar())!=EOF && c!='\n'; i++ )
    if( c!='\t' ) s[i] = c;
    else s[i] = ' ';
or,
for( i=0; (c=getchar())!=EOF && c!='\n'; i++ )
    s[i] = c!='\t' ? c : ' ';
```

Finally, it is clear that s[i] gets the next character if the character is not a tab, otherwise it gets a space. In other words, the code merely replaces tabs by spaces. The last two versions show this quite clearly while also pointing out the close relationship of the if statement to the conditional expression. In this example, the if emphasizes the test for tab and the conditional emphasizes the assignment to s[i].

Programming Style 2.5

```
if( j>k ) y = j / (x!=0 ? x : NEARZERO);
else y = k / (x!=0 ? x : NEARZERO);
```

In this problem it is quite clear that x!=0 is not the primary idea; the test simply protects against division by zero. The conditional nicely subordinates the zero check.

```
y = MAX(j,k) / (x!=0 ? x : NEARZERO);
```

A case can be made that the assignment to y is the primary idea, subordinating both tests. (MAX returns the greater of its two arguments.)

Storage Classes 1.1

`int i=0;`	i.0 = 0 (The notation x.*n* is used to refer to the variable x defined at block level *n*.†) The storage class of i.0 is `extern`.‡ The scope of i.0 is potentially any module loaded with this file. The lifetime of i.0 is the full execution time of this program.
`main ()`	
`{`	Block level is now 1.
`auto int i=1`	i.1 = 1 (i at level 1). The storage class of i.1 is `auto`. The scope of i.1 is the function `main`. The lifetime of i.1 is the duration of the execution of `main`.
`PRINT1 (d, i.1);`	When two variables have the same name, the innermost variable is referenced when the name is given; the outer variable is not directly accessible.
`{`	Block level is now 2.
`int i=2`	i.2 = 2. The storage class of i.2 is `auto`, the default storage class for variables defined in block 1 or higher. The scope of i.2 is block 2 and its lifetime is the duration of execution of block 2.
`PRINT1 (d, i.2);`	
`{`	Block level is now 3.
`i.2+=1`	i.2 = 3.
`PRINT1 (d, i.2);`	i.2 is printed since it is the innermost variable named i.
`}`	Block level returns to 2.

---

† The *block level* at any point in a program text is simply the count of left brackets ({) minus the count of right brackets (}). In other words, it is the number of textually open blocks. The outermost level of a program, no blocks open, is block level 0.

‡ You might ask why the storage class of i is not declared explicitly using the `extern` keyword. Unless declared otherwise, the storage class for variables defined at block level 0 is `extern`. Tagging a variable with `extern` does not define the variable. Instead, it tells the compiler that the variable has been defined elsewhere at block level 0.

`PRINT1(d,i.2);`	i.2 is printed again.
`}`	Block level returns to 1, i.2 dies.
`PRINT1(d,i.1);`	With the death of i.2, i.1 became the innermost variable named i.
`}`	Block level returns to 0.

Storage Classes 2.1

`int i=LOW;`	i.0 = 0.
`main ()`	
`{`	
`auto int i=HIGH;`	i.1 = 5.
`reset(i.1/2);`	The function `reset` is called with the value i.1/2, or 2. Its execution has no effect on i.1.
`PRINT1 (d,i.1)`	
`reset(i.1=i.1/2);`	`reset` is again called with i.1/2. This time i.1 is assigned 2 as a side effect of the function call. Again, `reset` has no effect on i.1.
`PRINT1 (d,i.1)`	
`i.1=reset(i.1/2)`	i.1 gets the value returned by `reset` called with i.1/2. We will expand the function call in line.
`int reset(int i)`	The type of the value returned by a function and any formal arguments are specified in its declaration. `reset` returns a value of type int and takes a single int argument.
`{ (int i.reset=1;)`	The formal augments of a function behave like local variables initialized to the value of their corresponding actual argument. We indicate these implied initializations by surrounding them with parentheses.
`i.reset = i.reset<=2 ? 5 : 2;`	i.reset = 5.
`return(i.reset);`	`reset` returns the integer 5, thus: i.1 = 5.
`}`	
`PRINT1 (d,i.1)`	
`workover(i.1);`	`workover` is passed the value of i.1; i.1 is not affected by the call. We'll expand `workover` since it includes a PRINT.

```
void workover(int i)
```

workover does not return a value so its return type is declared as void. (You may have noticed that workover is declared earlier in the file before the beginning of main. When a function is used before it is declared, it is assumed to have a return type of int.)

```
{ (i.workover=5;)

i.workover = 0 * whatever;
```

i.workover = 0.

```
PRINT1(d,i.workover);

}
```

```
PRINT1(d,i.1);

}
```

Storage Classes 3.1

```
int i=1;                          i.0 = 1.

main()

{

auto int i, j;                    i.1 and j.1 are defined, but not yet set.

i.1 = reset()                     i.1 gets the value returned by reset.

   int reset(void)                reset does not take any arguments so its
                                   formal argument list is declared void. Leaving
                                   the argument list empty, i.e., int reset(),
                                   disables type checking of calls to the function.

   {

      return(i.0)                 As reset has neither a formal argument nor a
                                   local variable named i, the reference to i must
                                   refer to i.0. reset returns 1, so i.1 = 1.

   }

for( j.1=1; j.1<3; j.1++ ) {      j.1 = 1.

PRINT2(d,i.1,j.1);

PRINT1(d,next(i.1));

   int next(int j)

   { (int j.next=1;)

      return(j.next=i.0++);       i.0 = 2 but next returns 1 since the
                                   increment occurs after the value of i.0 is taken.
                                   The return statement references i.0 since
                                   next knows of no other i. j.next dies with the
                                   return.

   }

PRINT1(d,last(i.1));

   int last(int j)

   { (int j.last=1;)

      static int i.last=10;       last has a local variable named i initialized to
                                   10. The storage class of i.last is static,
                                   which means that i.last is initialized when the
                                   program is loaded and dies when the program is
                                   terminated.
```

```
        return(j.last=i.last--);
```
i.last = 9 but 10 is returned since the decrement occurs after the value is taken.

j.last dies with the return, but i.last lives on. When last is called again, i.last will be 9.

```
    }
PRINT1(d,new(i.1+j.1));
    int new(int i)
    { (int i.new=2;)
    int j=10;
```
j.new = 10.

```
    return(i.new=j.new+=i.new);
```
j.new = 12, i.new = 12, and 12 is returned.

j.new and i.new die with the return.

```
    }
for( j.1=1; j.1<3; j.1++ ) {
```
j.1 = 2.
Back to the for statement. For this iteration we will generalize about the effect of each statement.

```
    PRINT2(d,i.1,j.1);
```
The effect of executing the loop body is to increment j.1 by one. The loop has no effect on the value of i.1.

```
    PRINT1(d,next(i.1));
```
next ignores the value it is passed and returns the current value of i.0. As a side effect of executing next, i.0 is incremented by one.

```
    PRINT1(d,last(i.1));
```
last also ignores the value of its passed argument. It returns the current value of its local static variable, i.last. As a side effect of executing last, i.last is decremented by one.

```
    PRINT1(d,new(i.1+j.1));
```
new returns the value of its argument plus 10. There are no lasting side effects.

```
    }
    }
```

Storage Classes 4.1

`int i=1;`	i.0 = 1.
`main()`	
`{`	
`auto int i,j;`	
`i.1 = reset()`	
`extern int i;`	The `extern` statement tells the compiler that i is an external variable defined elsewhere, possibly in another file. Here i refers to i.0.
`int reset(void)`	
`{`	
`return(i.0)`	i.0 is the external i referenced in `reset`. i.1=1.
`}`	
`for( j.1=1; j.1<3; j.1++ ){`	j.1 = 1.
`PRINT2(d,i.1,j.1);`	
`PRINT1(d,next());`	
`static int i=10;`	The second source file begins with an external definition of a variable named i. This definition might appear to be in conflict with the external variable i defined in the first file. The designation `static`, however, tells the compiler that this i is known only within the current file. In other words, it is only known within the functions next, last, and new. We will reference it by i.nln. i.nln=10.
`next(void)`	In the declaration of `next` the return type has been omitted. By default, functions have the return type `int`.

` return(i.nln+=1);`	i.nln = 11 and next returns 11.
` }`	
`PRINT1(d,last());`	
` last(void)`	
` return(i.nln-=1);`	i.nln = 10 and last returns 10. last references the same i previously incremented by next.
` }`	
`PRINT1(d,new(i.l+j.l));`	
` int new(int i)`	
` { (int i.new=2;)`	
` static int j=5;`	j.new = 5.
` return(i.new=j.new=5+2);`	j.new = 7, i.new = 7, and 7 is returned. i.nln is uneffected, i.new will die with the return, and j.new will be 7 when new is called again.
` }`	
`for( j.l=1; j.l<3; j.l++ ) {`	j.l = 2. In this iteration we will generalize about the effect of each statement.
`PRINT2(d,i.l,j.l);`	The effect of the loop is to increment j.l by one.
`PRINT1(d,next());`	next increments i.nln and returns the resulting value.
`PRINT1(d,last());`	last decrements i.nln and returns the resulting value.
`PRINT1(d,new(i.l+j.l));`	new adds its argument to j.new and returns the resulting sum.
` }`	
` }`	

Pointers and Arrays 1.1

`int a[] = {0,1,2,3,4}`	a is defined to be an array of five `int`s, with elements `a[i]=i` for i from 0 to 4.
`for( i=0; i<=4; i++ )`	i takes on the values 0 to 4.
`PR(d,a[i])`	`a[i]` accesses successively each element of a.

Pointers and Arrays 1.2

`int *p;`	Declarations of the form *type* `*x` tell the compiler that when `*x` appears in an expression it yields a value of type *type*. x is a pointer-to-*type* taking on values which are addresses of elements of type *type*. *Type* is the base type of x. In this problem, p is declared to be a pointer-to-`int`; the base type of p is int.
`for( p=&a[0];`	`&a[0]` evaluates to the address of `a[0]`.
`p<=&a[4];`	Array elements are stored in index order, that is, `a[0]` precedes `a[1]` precedes `a[2]` and so on. Thus p, initialized to `&a[0]`, is less than `&a[4]`.
`PR(d,*p);`	`*p` evaluates to the `int` stored at the address contained in p. Since p holds `&a[0]`, `*p` is `a[0]`.
`p++`	When applied to a pointer variable, the increment operator advances the pointer to the next element of its base type. What actually happens is that the pointer is incremented by `sizeof` (*base type*) bytes. C does not test to assure that the resulting address is really that of a valid element of the base type. In this problem, p++ advances p to the next element of a.
`p<=&a[4]`	p is again tested against the end of the array. The loop is terminated when p points beyond the last element of a. While in the loop, p points successively to each element of a in index order.

Pointers and Arrays 1.3

`for( p=&a[0],i=1; i<=5; i++ );`	p points to the start of the array a. i takes on the values 1 through 5.
`PR(d,p[i]);`	p[[i] refers successively to the elements of a. p[5] points outside of the array.

About arrays and indices. Though by far the most common use of [] is to represent array subscripting, [] actually is a general indexing operator. x[i] is defined to be *(x+i), where x is an address and i is integral. The rules of address arithmetic apply, so i is in units of sizeof(*base type* of x). (It should by now be clear why array indicies begin at 0. An array name is actually a pointer to the first element in the array. An index is the offset from the array start. The offset to the first element from the array start is 0.) In this last problem, i is used to index off p. p[i] = *(p+i) = *(a+i) = a[i]. i goes from 1 to 5. When i=5, p+i points just beyond the end of the array, hence the value at p+i is unknown. This is such a common mistake it is worth noting again: *an array with* n *elements has indicies of* 0 *through* n-1.

Pointers and Arrays 1.4

`for( p=a,i=0;`	p gets the address of the first element of a.
`p+i <= a+4;`	p=a, i=0, so p+i=a+0, which is less than a+4.
`PR(d,*(p+i));`	*(p+i) = *(a+0) = a[0].
`p++, i++`	p points to the second element of a, i is 1.
`p+i <= a+4`	p=a+1, i=1, p+i=a+2.
`PR(d,*(p+i))`	*(p+i) = a[2].
`p++, i++`	p=a+2, i=2.
`p+i <= a+4`	p+i = a+4.
`PR(d,*(p+i))`	*(p+i) = a[4].
`p++, i++`	p=a+3, i=3.
`p+i <= a+4`	p+i = a+6, and the loop terminates.

Pointers and Arrays 1.5

```
for( p=a+4;
```
p points to the fifth element of a.

```
p >= a;
```
The loop terminates when p points below a.

```
PR(d,*p);
```
The int pointed to by p is printed.

```
p--
```
p is decremented to the preceding element.

Pointers and Arrays 1.6

```
for( a+4,i=0; i<=4; i++ )
```
p points to the last element of a, i goes from 0 to 4.

```
PR(d,p[-i]);
```
The element −i away from the last element of a is printed.

Pointers and Arrays 1.7

```
for( p=a+4; p>=a; p-- )
```
p points successively to the elements of a from the last to the first.

```
PR(d,a[p-a]);
```
p−a evaluates to the offset from the start of the array to the element pointed to by p. In other words, p−a is the index of the element pointed to by p.

Pointers and Arrays 2.1

`int a[] = {0,1,2,3,4}`	a is initialized to be an array of five ints.
`int *p[] = {a,a+1,a+2,a+3,a+4};`	When encountered in an expression, `*p[]` evaluates to an int, thus `p[]` must point to an int, and p is an array of pointer-to-int. The five elements of p initially point to the five elements of a.
`int **pp = p;`	`**pp` evaluates to an int, hence `*pp` must point to an int, and pp must point to a pointer-to-int. pp initially points to `p[0]`.

Figure Point 2.1 illustrates the relationships between pp, p, and a.

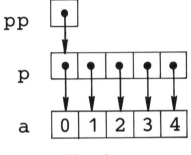

Figure 2.1

Pointers and Arrays 2.2

`PRINT2 (d, a, *a) ;`

As noted earlier, the name of an array is synonymous with the address of the first element in the array. The value of a is thus the address of the array a, and `*a` is equivalent to a [0].

`PRINT3 (d, p, *p, **p) ;`

p evaluates to the address of the first element of the array p. `*p` yields the value of p [0], and `**p` yields the int at the address contained in p [0], i.e., the value at a [0].

`PRINT3 (d, pp, *pp, **pp) ;`

pp yields the content of pp, the address of p. `**pp` yields the value at p, or p [0]. And `**pp` yields the int pointed to by p [0], a [0].

Pointers and Arrays 2.3

`pp++`

pp is a pointer to pointer-to-`int` (the base type of pp is pointer-to-`int`), so pp++ increments pp to point to the next pointer in memory. The effect of pp++ is indicated by the bold arrow in Figure 2.3-1.

`pp-p`

pp points to the second element of the array p, p [1]. The value of pp is thus p+1. pp-p = (p+1) -p, which is 1.

`*pp-a`

pp points to p [1] and `*pp` points to the second element of the array a. The value of `*pp` is thus a+1. `*pp-a` = (a+1) -a.

`**pp`

`**pp` points to a [1], so `**pp` yields the contents at a [1].

`*pp++`

`* (pp++)`
Unary operators group from right to left. First the increment is bound, then the indirection. The bold arrow in Figure 2.3-2 shows the effect of the increment.

`*++pp`

`* (++pp)`
(Figure 2.3-3)

`++*pp`

`++ (*pp)`
(Figure 2.3-4)

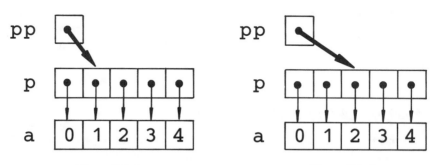

Figure 2.3-1

Figure 2.3-2

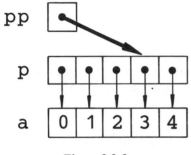

Figure 2.3-3

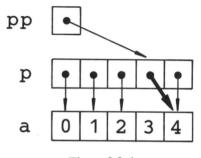

Figure 2.3-4

Pointers and Arrays 2.4

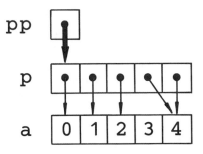

Figure 2.4-1 pp=p

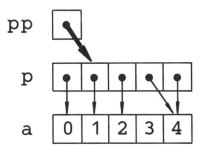

Figure 2.4-2 *(*(pp++))

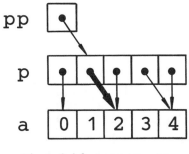

Figure 2.4-3 *(++(*pp))

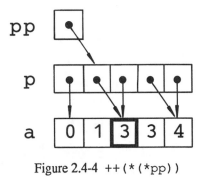

Figure 2.4-4 ++(*(*pp))

Pointers and Arrays 3.1

```
int a[3][3] = {
    { 1,2,3 },
    { 4,5,6 },
    { 7,8,9 }
};
```

a is a 3 by 3 matrix with rows 123, 456, and 789. a[i][j] evaluates to an int at offset j from the start of row i. a[i] yields the address of the first element of row i. And a yields the address of the first row of the matrix a. Thus a is a pointer to three-element-int-array, and a[] is pointer-to-int.

```
int *pa[3] = {
    a,a+1,&a[2]
};
```

*pa[] evaluates to an int, thus pa[] is a pointer-to-int and pa is an array of pointer-to-int. pa[0] is initialized to the first element of the first row of a, pa[1] to the first element in the second row, and pa[2] to the first element in the third row.

```
int *p = a;
```

p is a pointer-to-int pointing initially to the first element of the matrix a.

Figure Point 3.1 illustrates the relationships between a, pa, and p.

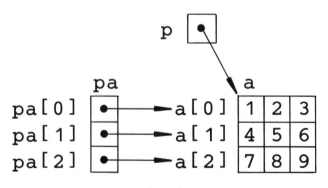

Figure 3.1

Pointers and Arrays 3.2

`for(i=0; i<3; i++)`	i goes from 0 to 2 in the loop.
`PRINT3(d,a[i][2-i],`	`a[i][2-i]` selects the diagonal from `a[0][2]` to `a[2][0]`.
`*a[i],`	`a[i]` yields the address of the first element of the ith row in the matrix a. `*a[i]` yields the value of the first element of the ith
`*(*(a+i)+i)`	`a+i` yields the address of the ith row of a. `*(a+i)` yields the address of the first element from the ith row. `*(a+i)+i` yields the address of the ith element from the ith row. And `*(*(a+i)+i)` gets the int value from the ith element of the ith row.

Pointers and Arrays 3.3

`for(i=0; i<3; i++)`	i goes from 0 to 2 in the loop.
`*pa[i]`	`pa[i]` accesses the ith element of pa. `*pa[i]` accesses the int pointed to by the ith element of pa.
`p[i]`	p points to the first element of the first row in the matrix a. Since the base type of p is int, `p[i]` yields the ith int of the first row in a.

About array addresses. We have noted several times that the address of an array and the address of the first element in the array have the same value. In this past puzzle, we saw that a and a[0] evaluated to the same address. One difference between the address of an array and the address of the first element in the array is the *type* of the address and, hence, the unit of arithmetic on an expression containing the address. Thus, since the type of a is pointer to three-element-int-array, the base type of a is three-element-int-array and a+1 refers to the next three-element-int-array in memory. Since the type of a[0] is pointer-to-int, the base type of a[0] is int and a[0]+1 refers to the next int in memory.

Pointers and Arrays 4.1

```
char *c[] = {
    "ENTER",
    "NEW",
    "POINT",
    "FIRST"
};
```

*c[] evaluates to a char, so c[] points to chars and c is an array of pointer-to-char. The elements of c have been initialized to point to the char arrays ENTER, NEW, POINT, and FIRST.

```
char **cp[] = {
    c+3, c+2, c+1, c
};
```

**cp[] evaluates to a char, *cp[] is a pointer-to-char, and cp[] is a pointer to pointer-to-char. Thus cp is an array of pointers to pointer-to-char. The elements of cp have been initialized to point to the elements of c.

```
char ***cpp = cp;
```

***cp evaluates to a char, **cp points to a char, *cp points to a pointer-to-char, and cp points to a pointer-to-pointer-to-char.

Figure Point 4.1 illustrates the relationships between cpp, cp, and c.

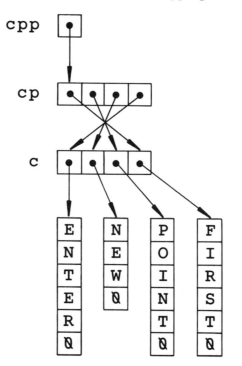

Figure 4.1

Pointers and Arrays 4.2

`*(*(++cpp))`	Increment cpp then follow the pointers. (Figure 4.2-1)
`(*(--(*(++cpp))))+3`	Increment cpp, follow the pointer to cp[2], decrement cp[2], follow the pointer to c[0], index 3 from the address in c[0]. (Figure 4.2-2)
`(*(cpp[(-2)]))+3`	Indirectly reference -2 from cpp yielding cp[0], follow the pointer to c[3], index 3 from the address in c[3]. (Figure 4.2-3)
`((cpp[-1])[-1])+1`	Indirectly reference -1 from cpp yielding cp[1], indirectly reference -1 from cp[1] yielding c[1], index 1 from the address in c[1]. (Figure 4.2-4)

About pointers. If you can work this puzzle correctly then you know everything you will ever need to about the mechanics of using pointers. The power of pointers lies in their generality: they can be chained together to form an endless variety of complex data structures. The danger of pointers lies in their power: complex pointer chains are seldom readable and even more seldom reliable.

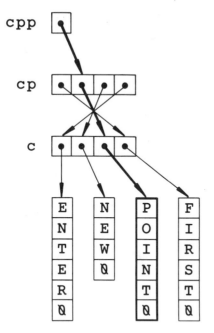

Figure 4.2-1

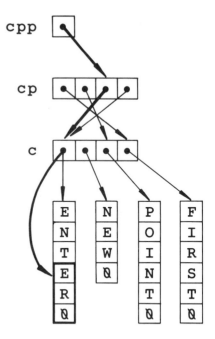

Figure 4.2-2

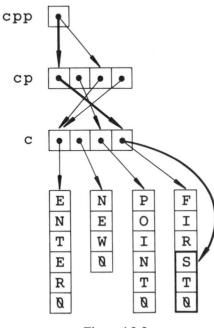

Figure 4.2-3

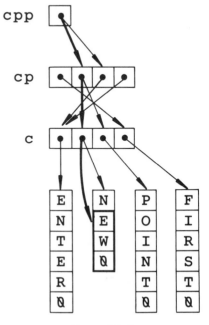

Figure 4.2-4

Structures 1.1

```
static struct S1 {
    char c[4], *s;
} s1 = { "abc", "def" };
```

The structure tag S1 refers to a structure containing a character array, c, of length 4, and a character pointer, s. The structure variable s1 is an instance of a struct S1 initialized to

```
        char  c[4]="abc",
              *s="def"
```

```
static struct S2 {
    char *cp;
    struct S1 ss1;
} s2 = { "ghi", { "jkl", "mno" } };
```

The structure tag S2 refers to a structure containing a character pointer, cp, and an instance of the structure S1, ss1. The structure variable s2 is an instance of the structure S2 initialized to

```
        char *cp="ghi";
        struct s1 ss1=
            {"jkl", "mno"};
```

Figure 1.1 depicts the structures s1 and s2.

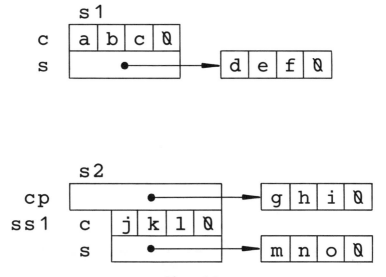

Figure 1.1

Structures 1.2

`PRINT2(c`	Print two characters.
`(s1.c)[0]`	Reference the first character of the c field of the structure s1. (Figure 1.2-1)
`*(s1.s)`	Reference the character pointed to by the s field of the structure s1. (Figure 1.2-2)

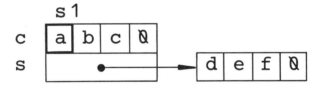

Figure 1.2-1

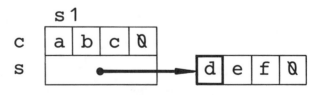

Figure 1.2-2

Structures 1.3

PRINT2(s   Print two strings.

s1.c   Reference the string pointed to by the c field of the structure s1. Recall that the name of an array is a reference to the first element, i.e., c= &c[0]. (Figure 1.3-1)

s1.s   Reference the string pointed to by the s field of the structure s1. (Figure 1.3-2)

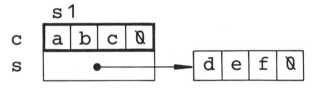

Figure 1.3-1

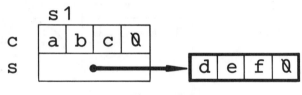

Figure 1.3-2

Structures 1.4

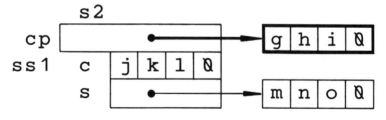

Figure 1.4-1   s2.cp

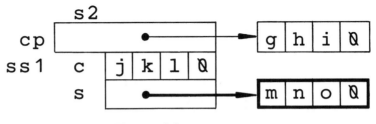

Figure 1.4-2   (s2.ss1).s

Structures 1.5

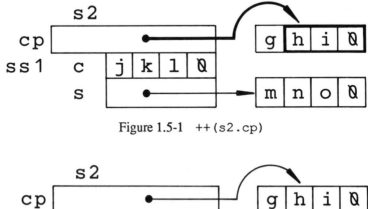

Figure 1.5-1   ++(s2.cp)

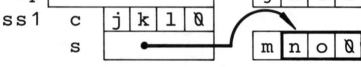

Figure 1.5-2   ++((s2.ss1).s)

Structures 2.1

```
struct S1 {
    char *s;
    int i;
    struct S1 *s1p;
};
```

S1 is declared to be a tag referring to a structure containing a character pointer, s, an integer, i, and a pointer to struct S1, s1p. This is only a declaration; an instance of a struct S1 is not created.

```
static struct S1 a[] = {
    { "abcd", 1, a+1 },
    { "efgh", 2, a+2 },
    { "ijkl", 3, a+3 }
};
```

a is a three-element array with elements of type struct S1.

```
struct S1 *p=a;
```

p is a pointer to struct S1. p is initialized to point to the first element of a.

Figure 2.1 depicts the array a and the pointer p.

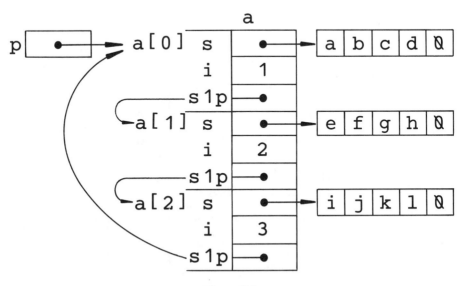

Figure 2.1

Structures 2.2

PRINT3(s	Print three strings.
(a[0]).s	Reference the string pointed to by the s field of the structure that is the first element of a. (Figure 2.2-1)
p->s	Reference the string pointed to by the s field of the structure pointed to by p. (Figure 2.2-2)
(((a[2]).s1p)->)s	Reference the string pointed to by the s field of the structure pointed to by the s1p field of the structure that is the third element of a. (Figure 2.2-3)

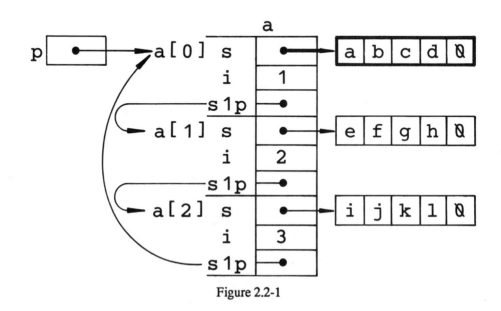

Figure 2.2-1

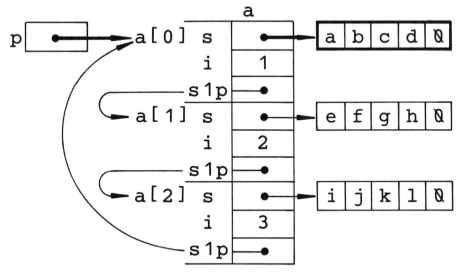

Figure 2.2-2

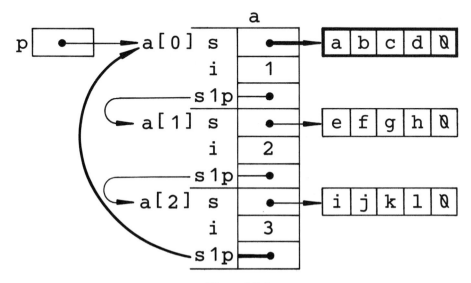

Figure 2.2-3

Structures 2.3

```
for( i=0; i<2; i++ ) {
```
i takes on the values 0 and 1.

```
PR(d
```
Print an integer.

```
--((a[i]).i)
```
Decrement then reference the integer in the i field of the structure that is the ith element of a. (Figure 2.3-1 shows the case for i=0)

```
PR(c
```
Print a character.

```
++(((a[i]).s)[3])
```
Increment then reference the fourth character of the string pointed to by the s field of the structure that is the ith element of a. (Figure 2.3-2 shows the case for i=0)

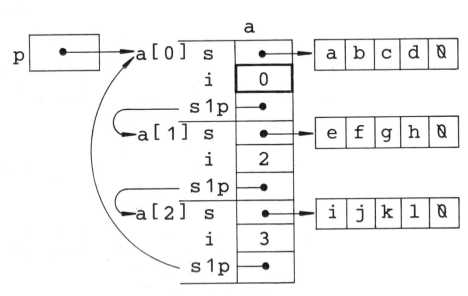

Figure 2.3-1

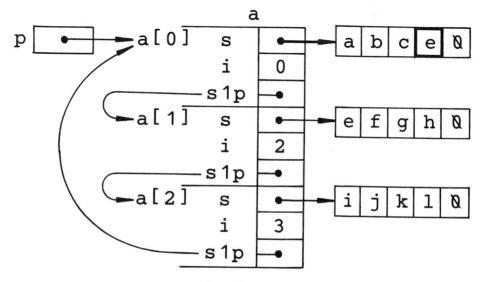

Figure 2.3-2

Structures 2.4

++(p->s)

Increment the s field of the structure pointed to by p, then output the string pointed to by the s field. (Figure 2.4-1)

(a[((++p)->i]).s

First p is incremented, then the s field of the p->ith structure of a is accessed. (Figure 2.4-2)

a[--((p->slp)->i)].s

The i field of the structure pointed to by the slp field of the structure pointed to by p is decremented then used as an index into a. (Figure 2.4-3)

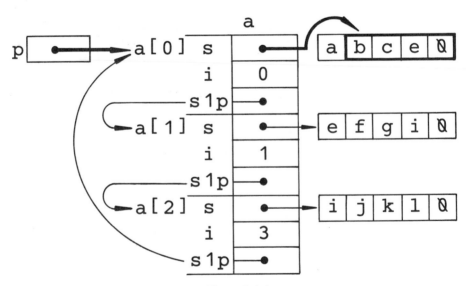

Figure 2.4-1

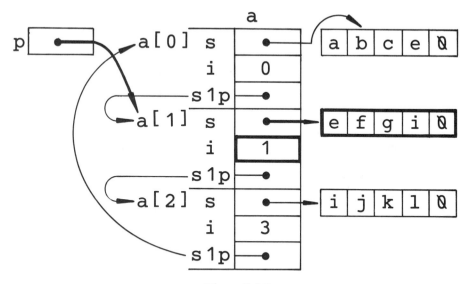

Figure 2.4-2

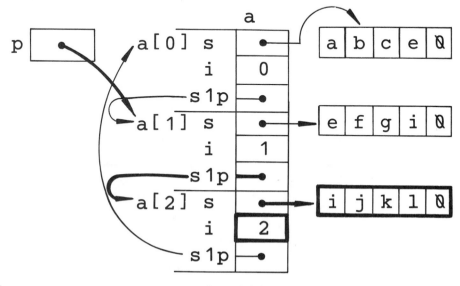

Figure 2.4-3

Structures 3.1

```
struct S1 {
    char *s;
    struct S1 *slp;
};
```

S1 is declared to be a tag referring to a structure containing a character pointer, s, and a pointer to a struct S1, slp.

```
static struct S1 a[] = {
    { "abcd", a+1 },
    { "efgh", a+2 },
    { "ijkl", a+3 }
};
```

a is a three-element array with elements of type struct S1.

```
struct S1 *(p[3]);
```

When encountered in a program statement, the expression *(p[]) yields a struct S1, thus p[] points to a struct S1, and p is a three-element array of pointers to struct S1.

Figure 3.1 depicts the arrays a and p.

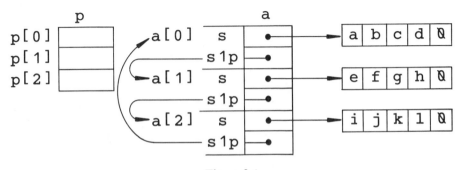

Figure 3.1

Structures 3.2

```
for( i=0; i<3; i++ )
```
i takes on the values 0, 1, 2.

```
p[i] = (a[i]).s1p
```
The i th element of p gets a copy of the pointer in the s1p field of the i th element of a. (Figure 3.2-1)

```
(p[0])->s, (*p)->s, (**p).s
```
These are all ways of saying the same thing. (Figure 3.2-2)

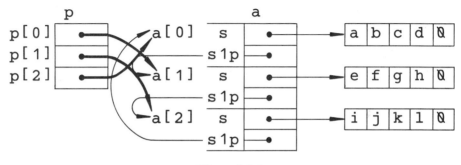

Figure 3.2-1

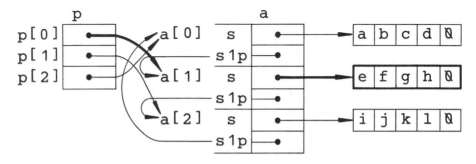

Figure 3.2-2

Structures 3.3

`swap(*p,a)`	p points to p[0], so *p yields the content of p[0] or &a[1]. a yields &a[0].
`temp = (&a[1])->s`	Equivalently, temp=a[1].s.
`(&a[1])->s = (&a[0])->s`	Or, a[1].s = a[0].s.
`(&a[0])->s = temp`	swap swaps the strings pointed to by the s fields of its arguments. (Figure 3.3-1)
`(p[0])->s, (*p)->s`	(Figure 3.3-2)
`((*p)->s1p)->s`	(Figure 3.3-3)

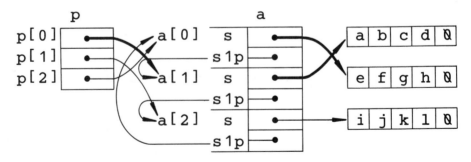

Figure 3.3-1

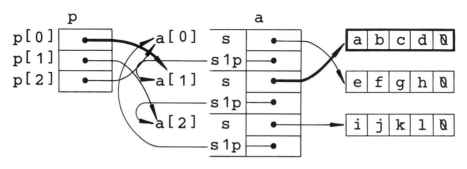

Figure 3.3-2

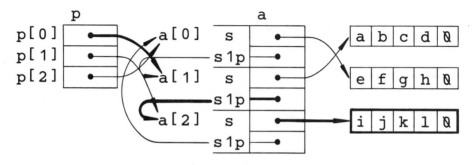

Figure 3.3-3

Structures 3.4

`swap(p[0], (p[0])->s1p)`   p[0] contains &a[1], (p[0])->s1p contains &a[2]. (Figure 3.4-1)

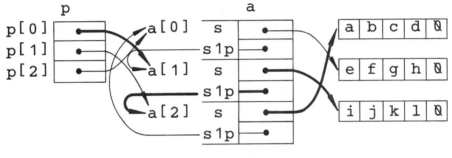

Figure 3.4-1

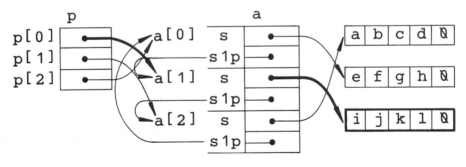

Figure 3.4-2   (p[0])->s

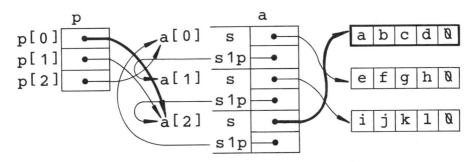

Figure 3.4-3   `(*(++(p[0]))).s`

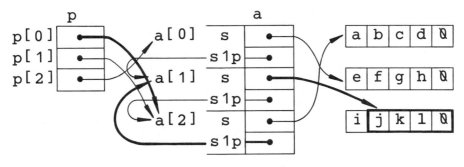

Figure 3.4-4   `++((*(++((*p)->s1p))).s)`

Preprocessor 1.1

`int x=2;` `PRINT( x*FUDGE(2) );`	To understand the effect of a macro, expand it in place.
`FUDGE(2)`	First expand any macros in the actual arguments.
`k+3.14159`	
`2+3.14159`	
`PRINT( x*2+3.14159 );`	Then substitute the expansion for the actual argument.
`PR(a); putchar('\n')`	Then expand the macro.
`PR(x*2+3.14159)`	Substitute the arguments.
`printf(#a " = %d\t",(int)a)`	Continue expanding and substituting until all macros have been processed.
`printf("x*2+3.14159" " = %d\t",` `   (int)x*2+3.14159)`	
`printf("x*2+3.14159" " = %d\t",` `   (int)x*2+3.14159); putchar('\n');`	Finally, replace the macro call by the resulting expansion. Surprise! The computation first multiplies then adds (then truncates).

Beware! Macros can be a source of subtle trickery. Expanding a macro is strictly a matter of replacing one token by another. The Preprocessor knows little about C. Most surprises can be avoided by adhering to a few conventions.

Convention 1: *Parenthesize all macro bodies that contain operators.*

The unwanted interaction between the replacement string and its context in this problem is avoided if `FUDGE(k)` is defined to be `(k+3.14159)`.

Preprocessor 1.2

```
for(cel=0; cel<=100; cel+=50)
    PRINT2 ( cel, 9.5/5*cel+32 );
```

```
for(cel=0; cel<=100; cel+=50)                    First expand the
    PR(cel);                                      call to PRINT2.
PRINT(9./5*cel+32);
```

```
for(cel=0; cel<=100; cel+=50)                    Then expand the
    printf("cel" " = %d\t",(int)cel);             call to PR.
PRINT(9./5*cel+32);
```

```
for(cel=0; cel<=100; cel+=50)                    Expand the call
    printf("cel" " = %d\t",(int)cel);             to PRINT.
PR(9./5*cel+32); putchar('\n');
```

```
for(cel=0; cel<=100; cel+=50)                    Expand the call
    printf("cel" " = %d\t",(int)cel);             to PR.
printf("9./5*cel+32" " = %d\t",(int)9./5*cel+32);
putchar('\n');
```

The call to PRINT2 may look like a single statement, but it expands to three. Only the first PR is contained within the for loop. The second PR is executed following the loop, with cel=150.

Convention 2: *Keep macro bodies cohesive; prefer an expression to a statement, a single statement to multiple statements.*

For this problem using commas in place of the semicolons in the body of the PRINT macros satisfies Convention 2.

Preprocessor 1.3

```
int x=1, y=2;
PRINT3 ( MAX(x++,y),x,y );
```

`(a<b ? b : a)`	Expand the call to MAX. (To avoid obscurring the point of the puzzles, in this and following solutions the PRINT macros will not be expanded.)
`(x++<y ? y : x++)`	Next, substitute the actual arguments for the formal arguments.
`(1<2 ? y : x++), and x=2`	Finally, evaluate.
`(y)`	
`2`	

`PRINT3 ( MAX(x++,y),x,y );`	Now execute the second call to PRINT3.
`(x++<y ? y : x++)`	
`(2<2 ? y : x++), and x=3`	
`(x++)`	
`3, and x=4`	

x++ appears only once in the macro call but twice in the expansion, causing x to be incremented sometimes by one and sometimes by two. The burden of protecting against side effects can be placed either with the macro writer or the macro user.

Convention 3: *Avoid macro bodies that can cause unobvious or inconsistent side effects.*
Convention 3A: *Avoid expressions with side effects in macro calls.*

In general, the problem of side effects in macros is quite tricky. Following Convention 3 often means copying arguments into local variables within the macro; this extra overhead reduces the speed advantage of the macro over a function call. Following Convention 3A requires knowing when a routine has been coded as a macro rather than as a function; at best, this violates the notion of the routine as an abstraction, and at worst, the routine may be rewritten causing the assumption no longer to be valid.

Preprocessor 2.1

```
PRINT( weeks(10080) )
```

```
(days(10080)/7)
```
Replace each macro call with the macro body. Notice that there is not a conflict between the macro parameter `mins` and the macro `mins`.

```
((hours(10080)/24)/7)
```

```
(((10080/60)/24)/7)
```

```
1
```
Evaluate.

```
PRINT( days(mins(86400)) )
```

```
days((secs/60))
```
Expand `mins`.

```
days((86400/60))
```
Substitute for `secs`.

```
(hours((86400/60))/24)
```
Expand `days`.

```
(((86400/60)/60)/24)
```
Expand `hours`.

```
1
```
Evaluate.

Preprocessor 2.2

```
int i;
traceon = 1;
for( i=20; i>0; i/=2 ) {
    if( i<10 ) TRACE(i);
    else puts("not yet");
}
```

```
if( i<10 )
    if(traceon)
        printf("Trace: "), PRINT(x);
    else puts("not yet");
```
`TRACE` includes an open `if` statement. On expansion the `if` consumes the following `else`. Thus the `puts` is called only when i<10 and !traceon.

Convention 4: *Make macro replacement strings complete C entities, be they expressions, statements (minus the closing semicolon), or blocks.*

For this problem appending a null else to the TRACE macro allieviates the difficulty. (Notice that enclosing the macro replacement string in braces, i.e., making it a block, does not solve the problem.)

About macros and functions Very often a routine can be implemented using either a macro or a function. The advantage of using a macro is that it will be executed faster since the runtime overhead of a function call is avoided. The advantages of using a function are that none of the tricky situations we've seen in the puzzles with macros will occur, and if the routine is called several times, the implementation will probably require less memory. This leads us to the final convention for using macros:

Convention 5: *Keep macros simple. If you can't keep a macro simple, make it a function.*

Preprocessor 2.3

```
puts ( g(oo,dbye) );

g(oo,dbye)

oo oo ## dbye(nd)                    Expanding g.

oo oodbye(nd)                        Before macros in the replacement string are
                                     expanded, the special Preprocessor
                                     operators # and ## are evaluated. ##
                                     concatenates its two operands.

"th" oodbye(nd)                      Expanding oo.

"th" "e e" # nd                      Expanding oodbye.

"th" "e e" "nd"                      Evaluating #.

"the end"                            The end.
```

APPENDICES

APPENDIX 1: Precedence Table

OPERATOR	ASSOCIATIVITY
primary: () [] -> .	left to right
unary: ! ~ ++ -- + - *(type)* * & sizeof	right to left
multiplicative: * / %	left to right
additive: + -	left to right
shift: << >>	left to right
relational: < <= > >=	left to right
equality: == !=	left to right
bitwise: &	left to right
bitwise: ^	left to right
bitwise: |	left to right
logical: &&	left to right
logical: ||	left to right
conditional: ?:	right to left
assignment: = += -= etc.	right to left
comma: ,	left to right

The precedence table illustrates the relative precedence of operators. Precedence determines the order in which operands are bound to operators. Operators receive their operands in order of decreasing operator precedence.

To determine the relative precedence of two operators in an expression find the operators in the OPERATOR column of the table. The operator higher in the list has the higher precedence. If the two operators are on the same line in the list, then look at the corresponding ASSOCIATIVITY entry. If it indicates "left to right", then the operator to the left in the expression has the higher precedence; if it indicates "right to left", then vice versa.

APPENDIX 2: Operator Summary Table

Arithmetic operators (operands are numbers and pointers)

- Addition

operator	yields	restrictions
$x+y$	sum of x and y	if either operand is a pointer the other must be integral†
$x-y$	difference of x less y	if either operand is a pointer the other must be integral or a pointer of the same base type

- Multiplication

operator	yields	restrictions
$x*y$	product of x and y	x, y must not be pointer
x/y	quotient of x divided by y	x, y must not be pointer
$x\%y$	remainder of dividing x by y	x, y must not be double, float, or pointer

---

† Integral stands for the types `int`, `char`, `short`, and `long`; both signed and unsigned.

- Sign

operator	yields	restrictions
$-x$	arithmetic negation of x	x must not be a pointer
$+x$	x	x must not be a pointer

- Increment

operator	yields	restrictions
x++ (x--)	x x is incremented (decremented) after use	x must be a reference to a numeric value or a pointer
++x (--x)	$x+1$ ($x-1$) x is incremented (decremented) before use	x must be a reference to a numeric value or a pointer

Assignment operators

operator	yields	restrictions
$x = y$	y cast in the type of x, x gets the value of y	x, y may be any type but array
x op= y	x op (y) cast in the type of x, x gets the value of x op (y)	x, y may be any type but array or structure

Bitwise operators (operands are integral)

- Logic

operator	yields	restrictions
$x \& y$	bit by bit AND of x and y; AND yields a 1 for each place both x and y have a 1, 0 otherwise	
$x \mid y$	bit by bit inclusive OR of x and y; inclusive OR yields a 0 for each place both x and y have a 0, 1 otherwise	
$x \char94 y$	bit by bit exclusive OR of x and y; exclusive OR yields a 0 for each place x and y have the same value, 1 otherwise	
$\tilde{}x$	one's-complement of x; 1s become 0s and 0s 1s	

- Shift

operator	yields	restrictions
$x<<y$	x left shifted y places, the lowest y bits get 0s	y must be positive and less than the number of bits per computer word
$x>>y$	x right shifted y places; the highest y bits get 0s for positive x, 1s or 0s depending on the compiler for negative x	y must be positive and less than the number of bits per computer word

Logic operators (operands are numbers and pointers)

operator	yields	restrictions
$x\&\&y$	AND of x and y: 1 if both x and y are nonzero, 0 otherwise	result is of type `int`
$x||y$	inclusive OR of x and y: 0 if both x and y are zero, 1 otherwise	result is of type `int`
$!x$	logical negation of x: 0 if x is nonzero, 1 otherwise	result is of type `int`

Comparison (operands are numbers and pointers)

· Relational

operator	yields	restrictions
$x<y$ $(x>y)$	1 if x is less than (greater than) y, 0 otherwise	result is of type `int`
$x<=y$ $(x>=y)$	1 if x is less than or equal to (greater than or equal to) y, 0 otherwise	result is of type `int`

· Equality

operator	yields	restrictions
$x==y$ $(x!=y)$	1 if x is equal to (not equal to) y, 0 otherwise	result is of type `int`

· Conditional

operator	yields	restrictions
$x?y:z$	y if x is nonzero, z otherwise	

Address operators

operator	yields	restrictions
$*x$	the value at the address contained in x cast in the base type of x	x must be a pointer
$\&x$	the address of x	x must be a reference to a value
$x[y]$	the value at the address $x+y$ cast in the base type of the address operand	one of the operands must be an address and the other must be integral
$x.y$	the value of the y field of the structure x	x must be a structure, y a structure field
$x\rightarrow y$	the value of the y field of the structure at the address x	x must be pointer to a structure, y a structure field

Type operators

operator	yields	restrictions
$(type)\,x$	x cast in the type $type$	x may be any expression
`sizeof` x	the size in bytes of x	x may be any expression
`sizeof(`$type$`)`	the size in bytes of an object of type $type$	

Sequence operator

operator	yields	restrictions
x,y	y x is evaluated before y	x, y may be any expression

APPENDIX 3: ASCII Table

In octal

```
|000 nul|001 soh|002 stx|003 etx|004 eot|005 enq|006 ack|007 bel|
|010 bs |011 ht |012 nl |013 vt |014 np |015 cr |016 so |017 si |
|020 dle|021 dc1|022 dc2|023 dc3|024 dc4|025 nak|026 syn|027 etb|
|030 can|031 em |032 sub|033 esc|034 fs |035 gs |036 rs |037 us |
|040 sp |041  ! |042  " |043  # |044  $ |045  % |046  & |047  ' |
|050  ( |051  ) |052  * |053  + |054  , |055  - |056  . |057  / |
|060  0 |061  1 |062  2 |063  3 |064  4 |065  5 |066  6 |067  7 |
|070  8 |071  9 |072  : |073  ; |074  < |075  = |076  > |077  ? |
|100  @ |101  A |102  B |103  C |104  D |105  E |106  F |107  G |
|110  H |111  I |112  J |113  K |114  L |115  M |116  N |117  O |
|120  P |121  Q |122  R |123  S |124  T |125  U |126  V |127  W |
|130  X |131  Y |132  Z |133  [ |134  \ |135  ] |136  ^ |137  _ |
|140  ` |141  a |142  b |143  c |144  d |145  e |146  f |147  g |
|150  h |151  i |152  j |153  k |154  l |155  m |156  n |157  o |
|160  p |161  q |162  r |163  s |164  t |165  u |166  v |167  w |
|170  x |171  y |172  z |173  { |174  | |175  } |176  ~ |177 del|
```

In decimal

```
|  0 nul|  1 soh|  2 stx|  3 etx|  4 eot|  5 enq|  6 ack|  7 bel|
|  8 bs |  9 ht | 10 nl | 11 vt | 12 np | 13 cr | 14 so | 15 si |
| 16 dle| 17 dc1| 18 dc2| 19 dc3| 20 dc4| 21 nak| 22 syn| 23 etb|
| 24 can| 25 em | 26 sub| 27 esc| 28 fs | 29 gs | 30 rs | 31 us |
| 32 sp | 33  ! | 34  " | 35  # | 36  $ | 37  % | 38  & | 39  ' |
| 40  ( | 41  ) | 42  * | 43  + | 44  , | 45  - | 46  . | 47  / |
| 48  0 | 49  1 | 50  2 | 51  3 | 52  4 | 53  5 | 54  6 | 55  7 |
| 56  8 | 57  9 | 58  : | 59  ; | 60  < | 61  = | 62  > | 63  ? |
| 64  @ | 65  A | 66  B | 67  C | 68  D | 69  E | 70  F | 71  G |
| 72  H | 73  I | 74  J | 75  K | 76  L | 77  M | 78  N | 79  O |
| 80  P | 81  Q | 82  R | 83  S | 84  T | 85  U | 86  V | 87  W |
| 88  X | 89  Y | 90  Z | 91  [ | 92  \ | 93  ] | 94  ^ | 95  _ |
| 96  ` | 97  a | 98  b | 99  c |100  d |101  e |102  f |103  g |
|104  h |105  i |106  j |107  k |108  l |109  m |110  n |111  o |
|112  p |113  q |114  r |115  s |116  t |117  u |118  v |119  w |
|120  x |121  y |122  z |123  { |124  | |125  } |126  ~ |127 del|
```

APPENDIX 4: Type Hierarchy Chart

```
long double
   ↑
double
   ↑
float
   ↑
unsigned long
   ↑
long
   ↑
unsigned int   (← unsigned short)
   ↑
int  ←   char, short
```

The type hierarchy chart illustrates the ordering of the arithmetic types. Before a binary arithmetic operator is evaluated, the two operands are converted to the type of the higher typed operand. The vertical arrows in the chart show the basic ordering: `long double` is the highest type, `int` the lowest. For any particular implementation, some of the levels may be identical; for example `long double` may be the same as `double` and `long` may be the same as `int`. The horizontal arrows indicate the automatic type conversions. That is, operands of type `char` and `short` are always converted to type `int` before being considered in an operation. An operand of type `unsigned short` is converted to `int` if its value can be represented in an `int`, otherwise it is converted to `unsigned int`.